I0458731

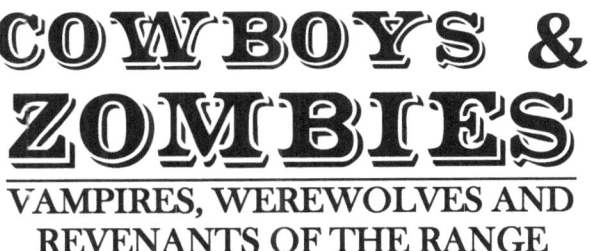

VAMPIRES, WEREWOLVES AND
REVENANTS OF THE RANGE

John LeMay

Bicep Books
Roswell, NM

First Edition

LeMay, John.
    Cowboys & Zombies: Vampires, Werewolves and
Revenants of the Range
    1. History—Pioneer Era. 2. Supernatural
    3. Folklore

HEADLESS HORSEMAN

Something at length appears to rouse from his reverie, and stimulate him to greater speed—his steed, at the same time. The latter, tossing up its head, gives utterance to a joyous neigh; and, with outstretched neck, and spread nostrils, advances in a gait gradually increasing to a canter. The proximity of the river explains the altered pace.

The horse halts not again, till the crystal current is surging against his flanks, and the legs of his rider are submerged knee-deep under the surface.

The animal eagerly assuages its thirst; crosses to the opposite side; and, with vigorous stride, ascends the sloping bank.

Upon the crest occurs a pause: as if the rider tarried till his steed should shake the water from its flanks. There is a rattling of saddle-flaps, and stirrup-leathers, resembling thunder, amidst a cloud of vapour, white as the spray of a cataract.

Out of this self-constituted *nimbus*, the Headless Horseman emerges; and moves onward, as before.

Apparently pricked by the spur, and guided by the rein, of his rider, the horse no longer strays from the track; but steps briskly forward, as if upon a path already trodden.

A treeless savannah stretches before—selvedged by the sky. Outlined against the azure is seen the imperfect centaurean shape gradually dissolving in the distance, till it becomes lost to view, under the mystic gleaming of the moonlight!*

*From Mayne Reid's *The Headless Horseman: A Strange Tale of Texas.*

EL MUERTO! THE HEADLESS ONE

For the Culz Paranormal crew

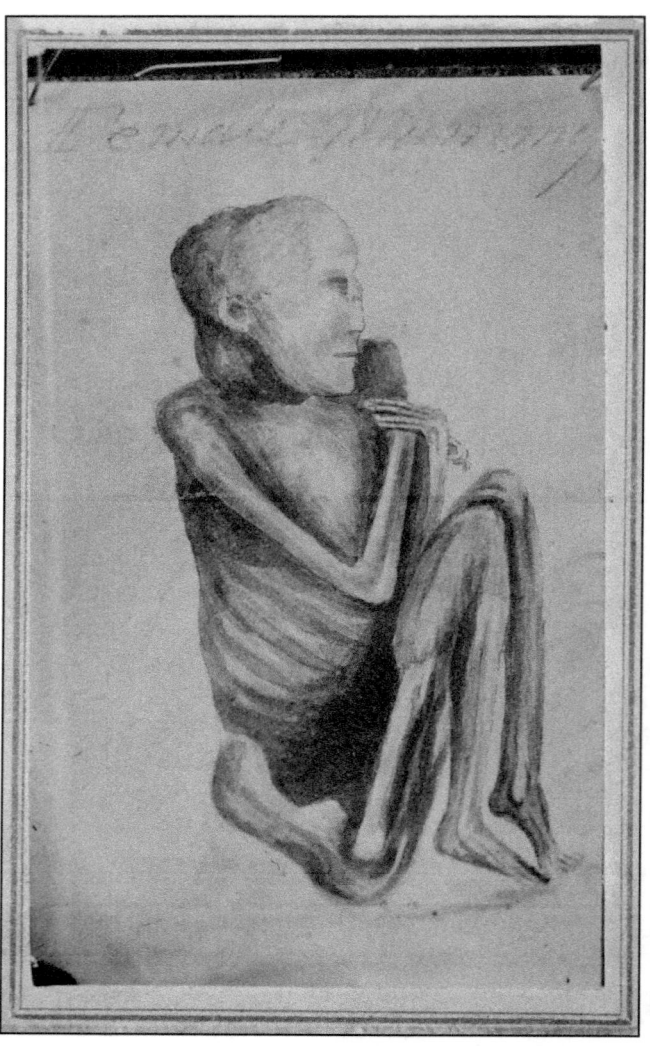

CONTENTS

INTRODUCTION   9

A SOMBER CANADIAN LEGEND.

The Story of a Human Being Assuming the Shape of a Wolf.

The werewolf legend constitutes one of the most somber of the traditionary beliefs existing in French Canada. The story of a human being assuming a wolf's shape is certainly one of the most generally diffused throughout the world and the werewolf story comes down to us from old Roman times. The French Canadian believes that if a person does not partake of the sacrament for seven years he will turn into a loup-garou—a shapeless animal without head or limbs; the loup-garou might also appropriate the form of a wildcat, a hare, a fox or even a black hen, but at night he was obliged to range through woods and desert places. At dead of night the loup-garou steals from his bed; climbing the highest tree in the neighborhood, he hides in its branches, and is instantly transformed into bestial shape. He is endowed with supernatural speed and strength. A fierce creature, with appetites exaggerating those of the animal he resembles, his especial delight is in slaughtering and devouring little children. When he returns to human semblance he may be recognized by his excessive leanness, wild eyes and haggard countenance. In order to regain his estate of humanity it is necessary that the blood of the monster should be shed. This kindly office being performed by a friend a complete restoration results.

INTRODUCTION
MORE MONSTERS OF THE WILD WEST

WHENEVER I START WORKING on a new book, I always do my best to include every story I possibly can relating to the subject matter. Every single time, there's always stuff I miss—and for that, I am glad. If not, I wouldn't be able to write another book. Since starting the *Cowboys & Saurians* series nearly ten years ago now, the fifth book, *Cowboys & Monsters: Vampires, Mummies, and Werewolves of the Wild West* has proven to be one of the more popular entries. This book comprises stories I missed on my first couple passes to chronicle all of the "monsters" of the Pioneer Period. In addition to vampires, mummies, and werewolves, one monster that got left out last time was that of the poor zombie, hence, the title of this tome.

Before doing *Cowboys & Monsters*, most of the books in this series had stuck to cryptids of the remnant dinosaur variety allegedly sighted during the Wild West, such as the fairly well-known Tombstone Thunderbird of 1890. By the second book, I had broadened my scope to include Ice Age megafauna—they, too, were prehistoric, after all. It was in the third entry, *Southerners & Saurians*, that I had included what sounded to be an 1892 sighting of the Lizard Man in South Carolina. Though reptilian, it didn't exactly qualify as prehistoric.

Perhaps it was that humanoid cryptid that opened the door for the fifth book, which chronicled more "traditional" humanoid monsters encountered in the Wild West in the form of vampires, werewolves, and even mummies. (Though, admittedly, none of the aforementioned mummies reanimated and came back to life.)

The book also illuminated versions of vampires and werewolves unique to the Southwest, namely the werewolf-like Skinwalkers of the Navajo and the vampiric Tlahuelpuchi of Tlaxcala, Mexico. Although it was never my intention to revisit these monsters in another entry in this series, as I was working on other titles, namely *The New Mexico Book of Witches*, I stumbled across more Skinwalker tales and Tlahuelpuchi-tangent stories. Stranger yet, in doing a few tomes on buried gold, I came across accounts of undead treasure guardians that sounded very much like zombies. After a while, it became clear that the monsters of the Wild West needed one more round, this time with zombies.

That said, as with the original *Cowboys & Monsters*, I did my best to avoid simple ghost tales unless something made them stand out—such as the specter that haunted Jesse James or the ghost rider version of Billy the Kid. I basically kept the same rule in this volume: No general ghosts unless they had fantastic, zombie-like attributes. The Headless Horseman of Texas, El Muerto, is a good example. Actually, El Muerto, the Dead One, was a true revenant in the sense that he was sighted in flesh and blood form as opposed to an incorporeal ghost. A few of his other headless kith and kin, likewise, had more in common with zombies than they did ghosts as well. With a few accounts of reanimated corpses to round out the book, I felt like the "Cowboys & Zombies" title was justified, even if none of them shambled about on a quest for human flesh as seen in modern cinema.

So, get ready for another supernatural sampling of mummies, zombie-like revenants, vampiric beings, shapeshifting Skinwalkers and an appendix of yet more humanoid monsters that defied categorization altogether. As with the others in this series, I hope it has what you're looking for.

John LeMay
Roswell, N.M.
November 17, 2024

In Twenty Parts, Sixpence each,

THE

HEADLESS HORSEMAN:

A STRANGE TALE OF TEXAS.

By CAPTAIN MAYNE REID.

CHAPMAN AND HALL, PICCADILLY.

Part I.]   [March 1.

CHAPTER I
HEADLESS HORSEMAN OF TEXAS

WHILE IT'S DEBATABLE whether or not a headless horseman really haunted Texas in ghost form, it's at least widely agreed upon that the basis for the story itself, along with its principal players, was real. For instance, Texas historian and newspaper columnist Ed Syers went on the trail of the Headless Horseman in the early 1960s and dug up some of the more detailed accounts of the incident from old-timers. His principal source was veteran gunsmith, Al Kennedy, of Ingram, Texas, who knew the tale "as well as anybody except those who occupy the three widely-separated graves he can take you to."[1]

---

[1] Syers, "Headless Horseman Rode in Texas," *Corpus Christi Times* (March 23, 1962).

BIGFOOT WALLACE c.1872.

The aforementioned graves belonged to particulars Bigfoot Wallace, Creed Taylor, and the Headless Horseman himself, buried near a little settlement called Ben Bolt outside of Corpus Christi. Furthermore, Kennedy claimed to have gotten his rendition from Creed Taylor himself before he died in 1906.

Captain Creed Taylor,

CREED TAYLOR IN HIS LATER YEARS.

Before diving headfirst into the tale of the headless one, some context is necessary. The story of the Headless Horseman, also known as *El Muerto* ("The Dead One"), began in the aftermath of the Mexican-American War of the late 1840s. The war, which roughly lasted for two years between 1846-1848, was fought over the nebulous border between Texas and Mexico. It was in this area that the ghost was born, so to speak. Appropriately, it was known as No Man's Land because, prior to the Mexican-American War, the U.S. regarded the Rio Grande as the border, while Mexico insisted the border was defined by the Nueces River to the north. Therefore, the land between the Nueces and the Rio Grande was No Man's Land, where lawlessness reigned before, during, and even after the war concluded. In particular, No Man's Land was a favorite spot for cattle rustlers from Mexico.

THE BATTLE OF PALO ALTO, DEPICTED ABOVE, WAS THE FIRST MAJOR BATTLE IN THE MEXICAN-AMERICAN WAR AND TOOK PLACE ON MAY 8, 1846, IN "NO MAN'S LAND" BETWEEN THE NUECES AND THE RIO GRANDE.

In 1850, an outlaw known only as Vidal was one of the most wanted cattle rustlers in Texas. While Texans were suffering a particularly bad Comanche raid, Vidal, along with three of his men, ingeniously took advantage of the ranchers' distraction along the San Antonio River to steal horses. Vidal's fatal mistake was the theft of some prized mustangs belonging to Texas Ranger Creed Taylor. However, Vidal only assumed Creed was off fighting the Comanche. In fact, he was still in the area, and quickly hit the trail in search of his missing mustangs along with another rancher named Flores. It was just the duo's luck that they happened to come across fellow Texas Ranger and legendary Mexican-American War veteran General William "Bigfoot" Wallace on the trail. In Syer's words, Wallace "was looking for the outlaw [Vidal] in general and any old excitement in particular."[2]

The three men found Vidal's outlaw camp that night, and laid in wait for a surprise attack in the dark. They crawled on their bellies through the tall grass, and by most accounts, they subdued Vidal and his men as easily as shooting fish in a barrel in the early morning hours. Taylor and Wallace wanted to make an example out of Vidal as one of Texas's most wanted. In the past, rustlers had been dealt with in brutal manners, such as chopping their dead bodies up into pieces and feeding them to the vultures. For Vidal, they wished a special send off.

Syer's, per Al Kennedy, said it was Wallace's idea in remembering the Washington Irving story about Ichabod Crane and the Headless Horseman, *The Legend of Sleepy Hollow*. And, although the men could have brought in Vidal's body and collected a

---

[2] Ibid.

reward, they still decided to forgo it in the interest of something far more dramatic.

... prayers and curses attended his ride

CORPUS CHRISTI TIMES (MARCH 23, 1962).

After killing Vidal, they chopped his head off and mounted his headless body onto the "strongest, wildest mustang in the herd." After saddling the horse, they "lashed the headless man to his mount," and "bound his hands to the pommel" so the body wouldn't fall off. Then, with a piece of rawhide which they "worked through the chin and jawbones" they attached Vidal's severed head, complete with the sombrero, to the saddle so that it jostled to and fro as the horse bolted off.[3]

---

[3] Ibid.

COWBOYS & ZOMBIES

Per Syers' article, "They cut loose the mustang. For five full minutes he fought his rider, but the horseman was up to stay—as the three avengers figured: A warning to rustlers. The mustang broke for the horizon."[4]

It worked, for several witnesses reported seeing the headless rider, not as a ghost; but as the actual corpse riding the horse. Some accounts stated that a few cowboys, thinking it was a headless ghost, shot at it, filling the body with holes before the poor mustang could run away. Due to the fact that the rigid body, tied to the saddle, never toppled over, they thought the headless rider was unkillable. One day, some ranchers from the little community of Ben Bolt, south of Alice, Texas, spotted the poor mustang at a watering hole with the dead rider still on its back. They captured it and finally freed the horse of the dead outlaw, whose corpse was indeed riddled with bullets.

Kennedy told Syers, "Finally, they got the horse at a water hole. Some say with a rope, some say with a gun. Vidal's body was pretty near a mummy, and it was a sieve with bullet holes."[5]

As stated before, Vidal finally received a proper burial somewhere near Ben Bolt, and the mustang was set free (in most versions, at least). "It's a legend from there," said Kennedy. "He was 'El Muerto del Rodeo'—the wandering dead you couldn't kill."[6] It was only later that witnesses would

---

[4] Ibid.
[5] Ibid.
[6] Ibid.

claim to see the corpse reanimated and riding the horse under its own power. After that, any bad luck in the borderlands was attributed to the headless rider.

At Fort Inge, near present-day Uvalde, soldiers began spotting the dead rider's ghost, still headless and atop the horse. Most reports said they were among the first to see the ghost, while other accounts specified that they saw the corpse in corporeal form prior to the capture of the mustang near Ben Bolt. In any case, cowboys across many parts the borderlands began spotting the ghost. One Texas cowpoke was so spooked by the sight of El Muerto, per the lore, he kept riding until he reached the state of Kansas, never to return.

DRAWING OF FORT INGE c.1867.

One of the more prominent sightings was had by a couple on their way to San Diego in their covered wagon in 1917. Just outside of their destination, they had to stop and make camp because it was getting late. That night they saw a huge gray stallion speed by with a headless man who shouted, "It is mine! It is all mine!"

COWBOYS & ZOMBIES

When Syers hit the trail of the headless horseman with Kennedy, he was curious how many people in what was formerly known as "No Man's Land" still saw the Headless Horseman. As the duo drove to the lonely rancher's cemetery outside of Ben Bolt, known as La Trinidad Cemeterio, Syers stopped at a remote gas station. As the old man that owned the station filled their tank, Kennedy asked him about the headless rider. The old-timer responded that mostly only the "old ones" spoke of him.

"They say that he still rides at nights," Kennedy said to the old man as he counted back their change. "To those who see him," he answered, simply.[7] Thus concluded Syer's article, too.

The ghost was seen after Syer's article of 1962, as other writers on the subject spoke of a significant sighting near Freer, Texas, in 1969. (However, none of them offer specifics as to the sighting.) One modern account said that witnesses claimed that "the horse spouted flames from its nostrils and sent lightning bolts skyward with each clop from its hooves." They also said that the "eyes in the head under the tattered sombrero were said to be like two fiery coals chipped from the cinders of hell." In these renditions, the Headless Horseman also gave off an eerie green glow and "smelled like brimstone as it thundered through the tumbleweeds and desert sage."[8]

---

[7] Ibid.
[8] In "Evolution of a Legend," author Lou Ann Herda referenced www.theoutlaws.com, which no longer exists.

JOHN LEMAY

ILLUSTRATION FROM THE FIRST EDITION OF
THE HEADLESS HORSEMAN:
A STRANGE TALE OF TEXAS
BY MAYNE REID, PUBLISHED IN 1865.

COWBOYS & ZOMBIES

As is usually the case in folktales, the commonly given rendition of the Headless Horseman is not the true-life version. Like a game of telephone, it had been misconstrued over the years. While most of the particulars of the story are still thought of as accurate, some of the participants didn't actually take part in it. As it turns out, while Creed Taylor did tell the story, he never placed himself in it. Others did that for him in later years.

Texas historian J. Warren Hunter first heard the story from Taylor at his home in Kimble County in the late 1880s. Hunter, to his credit, got the story right in his biography of Taylor entitled *The Life of Creed Taylor, Eighty-Six Years on the Texas Frontier* and published a decade later in 1898. Taylor's rendition included an alternate name for the rustler, Vuavis.

PAINTING OF THE SIEGE OF BEXAR.

Taylor knew the real name because he had met the man during the Siege of Bexar in late 1835. Lieutenant Vuavis had been a defector who informed on the Mexican army to Texas. Vuavis was serving under General Adrián Woll's command when he was captured. Vuavis offered information about Woll's future plans if they would spare his life, and they did. However, many years later, Vuavis had become the dreaded rustler known as Vidal.

Taylor's rendition of the killing of Vidal notably placed the events in 1848, not 1850, and the man to accompany Bigfoot Wallace was a Texas Ranger who had fought at the Battle of San Jacinto named John McPeters. Taylor said that Vidal and his men were killed at an encampment along the Nueces River, south of where Uvalde is today. Taylor was more specific in his account, stating that Wallace and McPeters caught the wild mustang and tied it between two trees as they mounted the body. Taylor specified a little more clearly that they tied the sombrero to the head as well. Taylor's rendition kept that the body took a long time to deteriorate and, other than the missing head, appeared life-like. (Oddly enough, Taylor claimed that the body became mummified and well-preserved due to Vidal's diet of chili and garlic!) Also, Taylor made it clear that the Fort Inge sightings occurred before Vidal was buried:

I heard afterwards, in fact Wallace was my informant, that soldiers at Fort Inge were greatly wrought up on seeing a man without a head, mounted on a superb stallion galloping around the country, scaring the life out of Indians and Mexicans, and frightening scouts and the few settlers out of their wits, and that they finally killed the horse by laying in wait at a watering place and shooting him . . ."[9]

To the best of anyone's knowledge, Bigfoot Wallace himself never told this story, which seemed odd as he loved to tell stories. In her essay, "Evolution of a Legend," author Lou Ann Herda noted that, "Strangely enough, though, neither John Duval nor A. J. Sowell, who each listened to Wallace's stories and wrote about his life in Texas, included this most curious crime in his biographies."[10]

ANOTHER ILLUSTRATION FROM *THE HEADLESS HORSEMAN: A STRANGE TALE OF TEXAS.*

It was Herda, as the name of her essay suggested, who successfully traced the lineage of the Headless

---

[9] Herda, "Evolution of a Legend," *Both Sides of the Border*, p.105.
[10] Ibid.

Horseman in print, and explained how Taylor's original tale got so misconstrued. The Headless Horseman's first foray into print was epic, and came in the form of Mayne Reid's 1866 novel *The Headless Horseman: A Strange Tale of Texas*. Supposedly, Reid had been stationed at Fort Inge and picked up the story there from the soldiers. However, the characters in the novel were fictitious, and the Headless Horseman served as the backbone of the narrative, sans the likes of Creed Taylor and Bigfoot Wallace.

As to how the common rendition of the Headless Horseman came about, we must return to J. Warren Hunter's biography on Taylor. In the early 1900s, Hunter tried to interest publisher and writer James T. De Shields in buying his Taylor story to adapt into a novel.[11] Though he didn't turn it into a novel, he did buy the manuscript for nonfiction purposes. De Shields, for whatever reason, decided to place Taylor in the saga of Vidal directly rather than simply as narrator. The ghost next appeared in print in the August 1924 edition of *Frontier Times* where editor J. Marvin Hunter integrated Taylor into the tale as De Shields had done. J. Frank Dobie came next, and naturally did his part in popularizing the legend.[12]

---

[11] *Cynthia Ann Parker*, De Shields' historical novel, had gotten him much acclaim and attention, and his articles in the *Fort Worth Press* were well received.

[12] Dobie tried to tie the horseman up with lost treasure, claiming he was the treasure guardian of the "abandoned Candelaria Mission on the Nueces" and that occasionally some saw the ghost with gold coins.

COWBOYS & ZOMBIES

ILLUSTRATION FROM DOBIE'S
TALES OF OLD-TIME TEXAS.

From Dobie on, Taylor always participated in the hunt. However, even though Taylor never took part in the story, the tale he told has good pedigree, and evidence would seem to suggest that a dead, decapitated body was strapped to a horse in Texas in the mid-nineteenth century. Notably, when Lou Ann Herda asked Taylor's descendants about the story, they all attested to its veracity.

Sources:

Herda, Lou Ann. "Evolution of a Legend." *Both Sides of the Border: A Scattering of Texas Folklore.* Texas A&M University Press, 2004.

Syers, Ed. "Headless Horseman Rode in Texas..." *Corpus Christi Times* (March 23, 1962).

CHAPTER 2
THE SKULL-SNATCHING SKINWALKER

AT THE ONSET OF THE Twentieth Century, the lands of the Navajo were beset by a strange epidemic of witchcraft. Starting in 1897 and extending into 1899, an unknown ghoul was robbing graves in Arizona on both sides of the Little Colorado River. Because the Navajo were sometimes buried with their more precious possessions, it wasn't uncommon for grave robbers to exhume recent burials to steal valuable bracelets and other jewelry or totems. This was different, though. The thief was beheading the corpses and stealing the skulls for reasons unknown.

Everything changed when a fifteen-year-old Navajo girl, Ha'dezbah Haske, died in June of 1899 and her grave, too, was desecrated. Her twenty-year-old brother, Ned Haske, had found her headless body exhumed from its grave, a set of coyote tracks leading away from the scene of the crime. It was no doubt the work of a witch—a skinwalker who had taken on the form of a coyote to do the ghastly deed. It wasn't just at this grave, either. All the desecrated burials bore the marks of a coyote to and from the crimes. Though others before him had been too fearful of the witch to track it, like any good hero, Ned Haske took a stand. However, Haske was also not as superstitious as his brethren. In the words of the *Frontier Times* article that told his story, "[Haske] did not believe that a man, by putting on a cape made of coyote skins and padding his feet and hands with the paws of that slinking animal, could turn himself temporarily into a witch to do evil."[13]

As it was, there were no witnesses to the desecrations, only the brutal aftermath. Furthermore, it was a typical practice that only close family members knew where they buried their dead, lest a witch or a robber come along to vandalize the grave. Therefore, the witch must've been a trusted member of the community to find the graves so easily. Haske assumed that the culprit likely only padded his feet with coyote paws to mask his tracks back to a horse. But, to his surprise, when Haske followed the coyote tracks, which were "walking on hind feet," they never led back to a horse. Instead, he tracked the paw prints for two miles until they disappeared into more rocky

---

[13] Winslowe, "Cache of Skulls," *Frontier Times* (January 1967), p.10.

terrain. It would appear that the culprit was either going to a great deal of trouble to conceal his identity, or he really had transformed into a coyote.

VIEW OF THE LITTLE COLORADO RIVER FLOWING THROUGH SPECTER CHASM IN ARIZONA. (U.S. GEOLOGICAL SURVEY PHOTO, c.1923)

Before setting out to get revenge, Haske needed to see to it that his poor sister's body was reburied. However, the Navajo had a staunch fear of *chindi*, or ghosts. The task of reburying his sister would instead fall to a trusted Anglo friend, S.I. Richardson, who ran the nearby Wolf Trading Post. About the same age as Haske, being nineteen, the two had become friends. So, when Haske asked Richardson if he might rebury his sister, he obliged, understanding his friend's hesitation due to the chindi. Watching gratefully from a safe distance, Haske saw that his sister had been reburied by his friend, then set off to catch the witch.

"AT BREAKFAST - TYPICAL DESERT HOME OF THE NAVAJO INDIANS, NAVAJO RESERVATION, ARIZONA." (LIBRARY OF CONGRESS)

Returning home to Garces Mesa,[14] Haske began construction of a weapon with which to kill the ghoul. Just in case the man really was a supernatural skinwalker, Haske needed a bow made from one of the old war bows. After borrowing just such a bow from an old-timer, Haske went to work making silver tipped arrows—

---

[14] Garces Mesa, coincidentally, was one of the locations used in Tony Hillerman's *Dark Wind*. Hillerman often used the lore of the skinwalker in his popular mystery novels.

the only thing that could kill the monster.[15] With his weapon ready, now all Haske had to do was wait for another death. It didn't take long. When an old woman passed away, Haske positioned himself at her grave for ten nights watching for the monster. Oddly, it never came. The process repeated itself when an infant died and was buried. Again, Haske watched, but no man nor monster appeared.

As in many stories, the third time was the charm. "Old Man" Denetso had just been buried, and after three nights of watching, Haske was probably ready to give up. But, at sunset on the third day, the monster finally came. But was it a monster or man? *Frontier Times* reported,

...Haske saw an object approaching, hunched over on the ground. As it reached the grave, Haske's blood tingled cold. The monster wore coyote skins fashioned into a whole one. The man, and surely it was one, walked bent over, forearms extended downward but never touching the ground.[16]

---

[15] In writing *The New Mexico Book of Witches*, I learned a great deal about the real-life folkloric methods of slaying monsters and witches. Oddly, silver bullets were more popular in the movies than in real-life folklore and custom. I never found any mention of silver bullets in relation to skinwalkers, so some part of me has to wonder if the silver-tipped arrows were a flourish added in by the *Frontier Times* author, who wrote the piece in the 1960s when werewolf movies were firmly embedded in the public consciousness.

[16] Winslowe, "Cache of Skulls," *Frontier Times* (January 1967), p.11.

Haske watched in horror as the man-creature squatted down near the grave seeming to wait for total darkness before it began to dig with "both hands in his coyote paw pads."[17] Not quite able to see the man-thing in the darkness aside from his shape, Haske took aim with a silver-tipped arrow. Somehow sensing his presence, the monster ceased its digging and turned to look at Haske. "The ears of the mask above his head" and "the pointed muzzle, were plain above the ground shadows," reported *Frontier Times*.

Haske shot the arrow, then heard a human scream. He had hit his target, who was now on the run. Despite being hit, Haske had watched the coyote-man leap away into the darkness in a feat of strength and agility that would seem more befitting of an animal than a man. Haske mounted his steed and took off in pursuit, but amazingly the man, if it was indeed a man, had vanished into the night without a trace. Satisfied that he had at least wounded the culprit, Haske rode back home to Garces Mesa.

Knowing that a silver-tipped arrow should have been fatal to a witch, Haske returned to the scene in daylight. As was the case at his sister's grave, he was able to follow the coyote tracks until once again, they disappeared onto rocky terrain. Haske did at least find a spot where the wounded man—creature, whatever it was—had stopped to remove the arrow. Along a wash, he found dried blood in

---

[17] Ibid.

a flat stone, and nearby, his silver-tipped arrow was buried hastily under some sand.

"MEDICINE MAN, PERFORMING HIS MYSTERIES OVER A DYING MAN" BY GEORGE CATLIN.

Eventually Haske went to the Wolf Trading Post to consult again with his friend Richardson. "One who is found wounded and who cannot explain how it happened, is your man," Richardson said.[18]

---

[18] Ibid.

With that, Haske waited for news of an area-resident succumbing to injury or death—silver was supposed to be fatal to this skinwalker, remember. While Richardson kept his ear to the ground at the trading post, Haske traveled about the country, visiting various hogans looking for injured men but finding none. Richardson's uncle, George McAdams, another prominent Navajo trader, got in on the hunt as well. When McAdams, who owned several trading posts, rode to check on one near Tuba City, he stopped to tell the local Indian agent, John Daw, of the desecrations occurring in the country along the Little Colorado River. Although Daw would conduct an investigation into the matter and turn up a few leads, it would still be Haske, with the help of Richardson, who would eventually end the monster's reign of terror.

Late one night, Haske and Richardson did some detective work of their own, determining that no less than 42 graves had been vandalized by the monster in the last two years. They also looked at a map of the area but could discern no patterns other than that all the crimes occurred in the vicinity of the Wolf Trading Post. They also noted that in none of the cases were turquoise or silver theft reported. Usually, a grave robber would dig up a grave, remove any precious jewelry, and then go sell them to a trader in another town or village. But no such thing had happened.

With no injured men to provide a lead, Haske turned his ear to rumors of men accused of witchcraft, one of which was a man called Nockitso, who hailed from Black Mountain. Haske made a severty-mile ride in vain when he found out that Nockitso had a firm alibi from his employer, whom he had been herding sheep for over the last six months and hadn't left the area.

POSTCARD DEPICTING THE TUBA CITY TRADING POST IN THE 1950s.

Complaining of his long trip for nothing to Richardson, Haske's friend told him he had heard rumors that an old man named Dugi-l'chee had recently offended several chindi, or ghosts. According to two customers at the trading post, Dugi-l'chee was constantly on the move due to these angry chindi. And why wouldn't chindi be angered if their resting places had been disturbed so vilely? Haske shook his head. It couldn't be Dugi-l'chee, as that was his uncle. And surely his uncle wouldn't vandalize the grave of his own niece.

As time marched on, the ghoul's depredations continued. It got so bad that families began burying their dead far away from where they lived in hopes the fiend couldn't find the graves. But, even as far away as Castle Buttes, forty miles east of Wolf Post, a dead man was disinterred and beheaded. And that was the real quandary: why the head? While Navajo witches were notorious for using dead body parts to make corpse powder, any part of the body would do. Fingertips, in particular, were highly prized due to the swirl-like pattern on them, and yet they went unmolested. An answer finally came when John Daw, acting as a tribal policeman, showed up at the Wolf Trading Post bearing a human scalp. It had been sold recently to a medicine man who lived at Willow Springs. The man who sold it was said to be none other than Nockitso, who was earlier cleared due to an alibi.

JOHN DAW, EARLY TRIBAL POLICEMAN.

BLACK MOUNTAIN, THE HOME OF THE SUSPECTED WITCH.

As it was, scalps were very valuable to medicine men in certain ceremonies and could be sold for anywhere between one to two hundred silver dollars at the time. At last, the case seemed to be solved. Nockitso was the one disinterring the graves, using the skinwalker's frightful methods to scare away the more superstitious. Daw went off to question Nockitso, who claimed that it was a Ute scalp, not a Navajo one, and that he had it in his possession for three years before he sold it to the medicine man at Willow Springs.

Unable to charge Nockitso, the matter had to be dropped. Luckily, a short time later, two policemen from Fort Defiance were riding the range when they came across two Ute men acting suspiciously. The men were searched, and found in their saddle rolls were three scalps, all Navajo. The men confessed that they had purchased the scalps from Nockitso.

One of the agents, Frank Walker, then went to the Indian agent at Tuba City, Robert E. Burris, and the two rode for Wolf Post and teamed with John Daw along the way. They questioned residents from the Wolf Post area all the way to Castle Buttes, but all the families were too afraid to admit to any knowledge of the witch. Eventually the trio went to see Richardson and showed him the scalps. One of them notably had a string of turquoise beads in the hair. He recognized it right away as having belonged to Ned Haske's sister.

Immediately, the men set off to arrest Nockitso, finally having proof of his crimes. Although Ned Haske was aware that the men were out to apprehend Nockitso, he wasn't taking any chances. At the same time, an old man by the name of Hosteen Redbird had died. His family had fled his hogan out of fear, due both to the man's chindi and also the skinwalker that would want his head. Haske arrived at the hogan, glad to see no coyote tracks around it... yet.

Haske laid in wait with his bow and arrows again. This time, he felt he would be successful. *Frontier Times* reported:

The ghoul didn't wait until nightfall. The sun was still nearly an hour high when Haske observed a furry coated figure approaching boldly through the purple sagebrush. It was indistinct and difficult to make out against the dun colored hummocks of the painted desert... Within minutes, he spotted the bent over figure trotting toward him carrying something in a dirty flour sack. Easily guessing its contents, Haske fitted a silver-tipped arrow to the bow. With careful aim from a kneeling position, Haske pulled the bowstring as far back as it would go.[19]

VINTAGE POSTCARD DEPICTING THE PAINTED DESERT NEAR TUBA CITY, AZ.

Unfortunately, again, something tipped the skinwalker off to the zooming arrow as it whooshed through the air. It dodged the would-be-fatal shot so that the arrow only struck the skinwalker in the shoulder. As it did last time, the man-thing darted away in a hurry, disappearing into a valley out of sight. Haske mounted his horse and gave chase, tracking the paw prints for over a mile and was still unable to catch up to the wounded ghoul.

Haske eventually tracked his prey to a location known as Burnt House Ruins, a spot once inhabited by the Anasazi along the Little Colorado

---

[19] Ibid, p.12.

River. The sun had by now set and it was dark. But Haske wasn't giving up. Along a dry wash, he saw evidence of recently moved sand and also a spade shovel. Haske dug into the earth knowing he would likely find the grisly severed head of poor old man Redbird. And indeed, he did, sans its scalp. Haske decided to rebury it, but as he was doing so, he came across more skulls. These ones were older, with the flesh having rotted off of them. This was it; the spot where the skinwalker was storing the skulls of its many victims at last.

NAVAJO HOGAN ON RESERVATION NEAR FLAGSTAFF ARIZONA

As a Navajo man, Haske naturally did not wish to stay near so many human remains. Besides, he couldn't lose his prey, not when he was so close. Somewhere in the darkness of Burnt House ruins was the witch. As Haske took a vantage point about a hundred feet away from the ruins, he saw the profile of the skinwalker slinking low to the ground.

COWBOYS & ZOMBIES

Haske readied his bow only to be shocked by gunfire. Although he had come prepared to deal with the witch via an ancient weapon, the skinwalker had turned the tables on him with modern firepower.

Haske cowered behind the rocks, hiding from any more gunshots. An hour passed of the tense, cat and mouse game in the moonlight, each man vying for a good spot to fire on the other. Finally, Haske picked up a rock and tossed it at the ruins. The witch opened fire; the light generated by the gunfire giving away his location against a high rock wall. The man, clearly thinking he had killed Haske, left his vantage point to investigate. As he did, Haske took note that the man had shed his animal skins and was dressed normally now.

Haske pulled back his bowstring and fired the silver-tipped arrow into the skinwalker's chest. The man screamed in pain and ran for the ruins where he collapsed. Confident he was down for the count, Haske followed him into the ruins. Strewn about the ground near the dead man was the coyote pelt plus poor Redbird's scalp. In the moonlight, Haske could also make out the face of his uncle, Dugi-l'chee. Sadly, Robertson had been right. Haske made the two-hour ride to Wolf Post and woke up his friend to give him the news. Within a few days, the tribal police also returned with Nockitso, who had confessed to buying the scalps from Dugi-l'chee all along.

In the end, Dugi-l'chee was buried near Burnt House ruins, the skulls were disinterred and properly reburied, and Nockitso was sentenced to only one year in jail. "Peace and quiet settled over the Little Colorado River around Wolf Post," the *Frontier Times* article began to conclude. "People were no longer afraid that their dead would be mutilated, or that a witch would endanger their lives at night if they moved abroad."[20]

The story, entitled "Cache of Skulls" in *Frontier Times'* January 1967 issue, was written by John R. Winslowe, in fact the pen name of Gladwell Richardson, none other than the son of S.I. Richardson. Gladwell was born four years after this story took place in 1903, and presumably his father told him the wild tale when he was old enough to hear it.[21] How well S.I. Richardson really remembered the events, or how much he chose to embellish them for the sake of his son, is, of course, debatable. Furthermore, why Richardson didn't want to lend authenticity to the tale by writing it under his real name is a bit curious. However, Richardson was such a prolific writer, he deliberately took on pen names so as not to oversaturate his own market. Notably he was also writing Western novels under his Winslowe penname at the same time he published the *Frontier Times* story.

---

[20] Ibid, p.68.

[21] Notably, Gladwell Richardson did not include any version of his "Cache of Skulls" article in his autobiography, *Navajo Trader*. The book did include a chapter on his own experiences with practitioners of witchcraft that occurred in the 1930s. Possibly, because Richardson didn't actually experience the story of Ned Haske himself, as it occurred in 1899, he didn't include it.

COWBOYS & ZOMBIES

GLADWELL RICHARDSON.

But back to the question at hand, that being, how much truth did the fantastic article really contain? Most likely the story was basically true but exaggerated in some way. While it's debatable whether or not certain Navajo witches truly transformed werewolf-style into predatory animals, that they donned animal skins to commit various depredations is fact. The only thing that really defied belief in the story was that on several occasions a man in a coyote skin was able to outpace a horse. Considering that Richardson claimed that the witch evaded Haske on horseback for over a mile during their final chase, then perhaps the man really had taken on a coyote form? After all, according to the Navajo of old and modern witnesses alike, skinwalkers are very, very fast.

Sources:

Winslowe, John R. "Cache of Skulls." *Frontier Times* (January 1967).

ZOMBIE ON A TRAIN?

Per the *Arizona Silver Belt* of March 31, 1910:

With an eastbound Santa Fe passenger train running at full speed out of Needles [California] yesterday the express agent and baggageman were so badly scared by the movements of a corpse in the baggage car that they would have deserted the car had it not been what is known as a blind baggage, according to the statement of a passenger who arrived here last night, says the Prescott Courier.

The corpse was being shipped from California to Ohio for interment. The body was that of a man who died four months ago. Soon after the train pulled out of Needles the occupants of the baggage car saw the lid of the box encasing the remains move, although it was sealed in the usual way. Aware that the man had been dead four months they were surprised at seeing such remarkable signs of life.

After recovering from the first shock they approached closer to the coffin casing and were further surprised to see the lid slowly rising from the box as if being pushed up by the strength of the body in the coffin. With the lid open the corpse continued to rise until almost in a standing position before the next station was reached, when with the aid of the trainmen the body was pushed back into its place and unloaded at the depot to be further prepared for shipment to its last resting place.

Passengers who saw the body claim that it was not scientifically prepared for shipment, judging from the odor, and that the box containing the coffin was not hermetically sealed strong enough to comply with the rules governing the shipment of corpses. The queer action of the corpse is believed to have been provoked by the warm weather prevailing in Needles and vicinity.

The paper's explanation that it was due to the weather was rather underwhelming to say the least!

CHAPTER 3
VAMPIRES
OF THE GREATER
SOUTHWEST

YES, THE OLD WEST had vampires just like old world Europe. Many of them were "brought" to the "New World" via the folklore and beliefs of European immigrants. While those alleged vampires adhered semi-closely to stories from the "Old World" with their crucifixes and stakes through the heart, the vampires of the American Southwest were of a different sort entirely. This is because they were born of a unique mix of beliefs stemming from the indigenous peoples, such as the Aztecs and various Native American tribes, plus the Spaniards, who arrived on the shores of Mexico in the 16th century.

Many of the "vampire stories" from the Southwest that I've stumbled across can be traced

ARTIST JOLYON YATES DEPICTION OF THE TLAHUELPUCHI.

to the Tlahuelpuchi of Tlaxcala, Mexico. Almost exclusively female, the Tlahuelpuchi would sit over a fire and remove its legs before turning into a bird of some kind. Then, it would fly from its abode to seek out an infant and drain it of its blood, not through vampiric teeth, but from a needle-like beak.

All manner of strange folkloric remedies existed to repel the creature, the oddest of which was surely to remove one's hat, then pin it to the ground with a knife in a circle. Somehow, this repelled the monster. However, more often than not, accused Tlahuelpuchi were simply stoned, burned, or beaten to death like any other accused witch. For that's what it really was in the minds of those who believed in it: a blood-drinking witch as opposed to an outright vampire.

And while we're on that tangent, it's important to note that in medieval times, there usually was no distinction between either a witch or a werewolf or a witch and a vampire. It was simply a given in most beliefs that witches often drank blood and could transform into animals if desired.

OTHER CENTRAL AMERICAN

VAMPIRES

A variation of the vampiric Tlahuelpuchi was the Teyollohcuani—the name literally meaning "To Eat Someone at the Heart." It, too, turned into an avian creature and preyed upon children in the night, sometimes eating their hearts rather than sucking their blood. Not coincidentally, it was found in the state of Puebla, next door to Tlaxcala. As opposed to owls or turkeys, the Teyollohcuani was associated with other birds depicted in pre-Columbian art that drank blood, particularly eagles and hummingbirds. Another variation was the Mometzcopinqui, meaning "she reproduces her own thighs." Like the Tlahuelpuchi, the witch removed her legs in an effort to decrease the size of her body before assuming avian form. However, the Mometzcopinqui replaced her legs with those of a turkey's. Instead of grabbing a turkey's wings, for some reason, she just got some woven mats to replace her arms with, which served as wings. Franciscan friar Bernardino de Sahagun related that such witches were born on the calendar day-sign of One Rain of the Aztecs. If a woman was born on the day of One Rain she would develop supernatural abilities and become a *Mometzcopinqui.*

That refresher on the Tlahuelpuchi was necessary because, as said before, many of the folktales about to be reprinted featured elements of the Tlahuelpuchi in them. Most of these stories came from an oft-neglected tome entitled *Hispanic Legends from New Mexico*, which hinged heavily upon ghosts, goblins, and a few vampiric creatures.

A story from San Pablo, New Mexico, south of Las Cruces, told of an owl-witch who was dispatched à la the Tlahuelpuchi, that being the throwing of a hat into an enchanted circle. It also integrated another obscure, folkloric method of dealing with a vampire from Europe: that of sprinkling seeds or other small objects outside of the vampire's grave. Due to their obsessive-compulsive nature, vampires would be compelled to pick up the seeds all night long until the sun rose and destroyed them. In full, the account read:

A man from San Pablo was cutting some timber in a nearby forest. For a good many days late in the evening he had been molested by an owl crying like a woman. He told his neighbors about the owl crying like a woman. One of the neighbors suggested that the owl was a witch. Another one told him to take with him some mustard seed. "Next time that you hear the owl, make a circle on the ground, scatter the mustard seed inside the circle, take three steps backward, and throw your hat in the circle."

The following day the man went on to his work as usual. About the same hour the owl began to cry like a woman. Soon the man left his work, made a big circle on the ground, scattered the mustard seeds, took three steps backward, and threw his hat into the circle. At once the owl flew into the circle and began to pick at the mustard seeds. The owl had picked at a few of the mustard seeds when suddenly it turned into a woman. She begged the man to let her go. She promised that she would never bother him again.[22]

Another story collected from somewhere in Colorado in 1953 also featured elements of Mexico's vampires. (Note: Although collected in 1953, the story was probably set in the past.) The account concerned two old men who believed a woman to be a witch, so they decided to spy on her home. As suspected, one night, she flew out of the house in the form of an owl. While she was gone, the men broke into the house to look around. Like the vampiric Tlahuelpuchi, she had detached her legs to take on her owl form: "In the bedroom they saw two human legs. One of the men went out of the house and was gone for a few minutes and, returning to the house, he brought a small crucifix and laid it on the bed where the two legs were. They went outside to see what would happen."[23]

---

[22] Robe, *Hispanic Legends from New Mexico*, p.335-36. Another story from page 374 also alluded to the OCD traits of vampires: "Witches eat bones of men from the graveyard, and they eat rice by picking up each grain separately with a toothpick."

[23] Ibid, p.373.

The owl soon returned but would not go back into the house. In fact, whenever it landed, it would fall on its side. Eventually, the witch began begging the men to go back inside and take the crucifix away from her bed. Either out of compassion or fear, they did as told and removed the cross. After that, the owl flew into the house and "changed into a lady and her legs came in contact with her body."

Another story in the book told of what appeared to be a headless vampire. It was collected in Capitan, New Mexico, famous as the home of the real Smokey Bear. It utilized the tried and true method of burning the vampire to destroy it:

> A man would get up every night and become headless. He had a white horse and would ride through the town, go into the homes of the people, kill them, and drink their blood. A man went to the home of the person thought to be the ghost and found him dead. The people burned his body and put his ashes in a box with a cross and he has never returned.[24]

---

[24] Ibid, p.80.

VIEW OF CAPITAN MOUNTAIN, FOR WHICH THE TOWN OF CAPITAN, NEW MEXICO, IS NAMED.

Another story printed in the book could have been entitled "The Vampire Baby of Santa Fe." It combined a popular folktale about a monstrous baby found on the roadside but gave the baby more vampiric traits than usual:

A certain young man had a girl. She lived on one side of town and he lived on the other. The shortest way to her house was through a cemetery. Every night he walked through it to see her. One night as he walked through the cemetery, he heard a baby cry. He thought nothing of it. Next night he heard it again, so he looked around for the sound. There, behind the tombstone lying on a grave, was a baby. He bent over it and the baby stopped crying and two fangs appeared.

"BILLY THE KID."

The man said, "Christ! What is it?" and the baby disappeared in a cloud of smoke.[25]

Even Billy the Kid, the famous outlaw, once told a folktale about a witch who could detach her limbs, though no vampiric attributes were applied to her. Billy heard it from a woman named Maria Candelaria, who said her great-uncle was walking by Doña Peipeiuta's home one night in the village of Le Febre when he witnessed something horrifying. He claimed that when he peeped into a window, he saw Doña Peipeiuta sitting on a wooden bench over a steaming tub of hot water. He watched with grotesque fascination as she took off one of her legs and washed it in the water, which boiled any time she submerged a limb in it. The man watched her do her arms as well, and it all became too much for him when she detached her head and began to scrub it in the tub as well.

---

[25] Ibid, p.163.

THE VAMPIRE BAT-MURDEROUS ATTACK ON A SLEEPING WOMAN, AT COQUIMBO CHILI

The following story, again from *Hispanic Legends from New Mexico*, could be considered within the realm of vampires due to the fact that the witch turned into a vampire bat at times. Some of the scenes that played out in the story would have been right at home in a Hammer vampire film, with the damsel in distress falling under a hypnotic spell when she is bitten on the neck. As in the movies, when the vampire is defeated, the damsel's wounds inflicted by the vampire are healed instantly. At the story's end, the witch even turns into a monstrous bat, making one wonder if the teller of the tale was inspired by Universal's horror films of the 1940s. It should be noted that the story was collected in 1952, although the old-timer who told it claimed his own father, who told it to him long ago, attested to it being a real event.

People of long ago believed in witches and once they started to tell stories they would never stop because they knew a lot of them. This happened about 100 years ago, since my great-grandfather's time. I cannot remember exactly the place it happened, but it was here in New Mexico.

Once a husband noticed that his wife was being pursued by a strange black shape that disappeared into the forest at night like a giant bat. One day he went home and sharpened his arrows and spears and started to hunt for his wife's tormentor until one twilight he saw that the bat had a human head and face. So he suspected a witch, an old woman who was very famous for casting spells and calling up dead spirits.

Night after night he trailed the witch without letting his wife know about it. At this time the old witch was supposed to be sound asleep in her hut, but her spirit had entered into the bodies of a bat and a black panther and, in those shapes, she was hunting for a victim, who was this husband's wife.

The husband went and built a huge net of strong rope. He wove the net under the new moon and had a medicine man say a good charm over the weaving. He then waited every night by the side of the house for something to happen, until finally one night his wife came out with her eyes closed, moaning as if she had a terrible pain. Her body and spirit were being called by the evil spirit who was waiting in the forest. He then followed her. Beyond the first tree a leopard shape dropped down from a bough and sank its teeth into the woman's throat. The husband at once threw the net over the woman and the leopard. As the coils of the net touched the leopard, it changed into a bat and then into an old woman, who was supposed to be asleep in the village.

The man released his wife and even the wound in her throat disappeared when the leopard changed into the witch herself. He took the witch woman into the village so that other people could witness too. When they released her from the net, her shape vanished until they roused the sleeping hag in her hut and touched her with the net.

At the first touch of the net the hag changed into a spitting leopard and finally into the huge winged bat. The bat was crushed and killed and, as the blood poured into the ground, it took the shape of the old hag.

It was claimed that she had been an old witch and that she was able to take the form of any animal to hunt her victims so that she could continue her own weird life with their warm blood.[26]

---

[26] Ibid, pp.247-48.

Horror Broadcast Scares El Paso

EL PASO, Dec. 10.—(UP)—A rumor that a "vampire man" was at large in El Paso was traced today to the broadcast of a three-act horror play over radio station XEJ in Juarez, Mexico, several weeks ago.

Lester Farber, president of the station, said Juarez citizens were talking about the "little girl who was killed by a vampire in El Paso."

"We are presenting a special program tonight to show that the rumor was unfounded," Farber said.

Stories such as these fostered a strong belief in vampires in the Southwest even into the 20th century, as evidenced by this story from the late 1930s. Everyone, of course, remembers the furor created over the 1938 Halloween broadcast of *War of the Worlds*. In that case, some people believed the radio play was actually happening in real-time, causing panic among many listeners. Lesser known was a smaller furor stirred up on the border in El Paso, Texas. In his article, "The Pre-War Monster Panics of 1938," Theo Paijmans related that, "Later [in 1938], rumours of a vampire who had murdered a young girl in El Paso surfaced around neighbouring Juarez, just over the Mexican border. An El Paso schoolteacher reported to the police that her pupils were greatly upset."

COWBOYS & ZOMBIES

I searched out articles on the incident myself and found a few, such as this one from the *El Paso Herald Post* of December 10, 1938:

Horror Broadcast Scares El Paso
EL PASO, Dec. 10 — (UP)—A rumor that a "vampire man" was at large in El Paso was traced today to the broadcast of a three-act horror play over radio station XEJ in Juarez, Mexico, several weeks ago.

Lester Farber, president of the station, said Juarez citizens were talking about the "little girl who was killed by a vampire in El Paso."

"We are presenting a special program tonight to show that the rumor was unfounded," Farber said.

While no actual vampires were afoot, the fact that a radio broadcast making that clear was necessary just went to show how steadfast the belief in the undead still was in the Southwest at that time.

Sources:
Kutz, Jack. *Mysteries & Miracles of New Mexico.* Rhombus Press, 1988.

Paijmans, Theo. "The Pre-War Monster Panics of 1938." *Fortean Times* (Blasts from the Past).

Robe, Stanley L. *Hispanic Legends from New Mexico (Folklore and Mythology Studies: 31).* University of California Press, 1980.

FIND PREHISTORIC MUMMY IN CLIFFS

A prehistoric mummy only 32 inches long, with 20 teeth instead of the usual 28, with three fingers on each hand and four toes on the left foot, —the right foot is missing entirely— was recently discover by Jack Wilson and Mrs. Dovey Smith in a cliff dwelling near Wilson's place, which is six miles above the Windmill ranch on the east side of the Verde.

Though a hundred or more mummified dwarfs have been found in the cliff dwellings along the Verde and Beaver creek, this is the first that has not had a full complement of fingers, toes and teeth. It is believed that he was a freak.

The mummy discovered by Wilson and Mrs. Smith was wrapped in coarse cotton cloth and had cotton which still contained seeds. It was determined long ago by scientists that the prehistoric races which inhabited this region grew cotton and wove cloth.

The right foot had been broken off and it has not yet been located. A number of other human bones are in the same cave and the missing foot may be among them.

Those who have examined the mummy, which is now at Wilson's farm, declare that the teeth are well formed and evidently those of an adult, thus disposing of the theory that the mummy may be the remains of an infant.

The head is well formed and it is believed that the owner was not a person of defective mentality, regardless of his stature and shortage of digits.

THE PHOENIX ARIZONA REPUBLICAN
OF MAY 1, 1922.

CHAPTER 4
MUMMIES OF
MONTEZUMA CASTLE

NEARLY EVERY CULTURE has a legend of the Little People, from the ancient Leprechauns of Ireland to the newer gremlins that originated in the early 20th century. These Little People, similar to but not to be confused with fairies, were always magical but mischievous. Lewis and Clark heard tales of devilish Little People in South Dakota during their famous expedition. Many years later, the body of one may have been found in the San Pedro Mountains of Wyoming in 1932.

The Southwest region has their Little People, too. The Spanish call them duendes, and the legend of their origin actually likens them to fallen angels. So the legend went, when Lucifer fell from Heaven and took a third of the angels with him, God shut Heaven's gates. The fallen angels who had already reached Earth below became demons, while the ones still falling in mid-air became the mischievous duendes. There are still honest New Mexicans and Arizonians to this day that attest that duendes are real; a few have even seen one.

ENGRAVING OF EUROPEAN DWARVES.

Aurelio M. Espinosa notably wrote of these dwarves in *The Journal of American Folklore* Vol. 23, No. 90 (Oct. - Dec., 1910):

Dwarfs (*los duendes*) are individuals of small stature, who frighten the lazy, the wicked, and in particular the filthy. The New Mexican idea about dwarfs is embraced in the above statement. The people express much uncertainty about the origin, whereabouts, and doings of dwarfs. A young lady from Santa Fe, however, seemed to have some definite ideas about their life. She pictured them as living together in a certain lonely place, where they inhabited underground houses, went out secretly to steal provisions and clothing, especially at night, and often even went to the cities to buy provisions. In the caves they prospered and lived with their families. Most of the people, however, profess ignorance about dwarfs. They have only the general idea of their being evil spirits that terrorize the wicked, lazy, or filthy, as I have already stated.[27]

The Mescalero Apache of New Mexico also knew of what could be considered the Duendes. An honest account of one was reprinted in Sherry Robinson's book *Apache Voices*. Specifically, the witness was Eugene Chihuahua, who told Eve Ball:

It was up on that high flat mountain where [Chief] Juh lived that I first saw one of the little people. I thought at first that he was another child about two or three years old and that he might be lost from his mother but when I got close I saw that he was a grown man, not a child. I told nobody but Daklugie and he explained. There are Little People living in the forest and they sometimes come around the outskirts of a rancheria [village] but never inside. They are not ghosts nor witches but just small people who never die. And they mean good to the Apaches."[28]

---

[27] Espinosa, *Journal of American Folklore*, p.399.
[28] Robinson, *Apache Voices*, p.184.

ACE DAKLUGIE, WHO EUGENE CHIHUAHUA
MENTIONED THE LITTLE PEOPLE TO.

As it turns out, while Chihuahua may have been wrong about the Little People never dying, evidence was found in Arizona proving that they may have existed in the Southwest, just like the San Pedro Mountains mummy. *The Phoenix Arizona Republican* published a story on the Arizona find on May 1, 1922:

COWBOYS & ZOMBIES

A prehistoric mummy only 32 inches long:, with 20 teeth instead of the usual 28, with three fingers on each hand and four toes on the left foot,—the right foot is missing entirely—was recently discover by Jack Wilson and Mrs. Dovey Smith in a cliff dwelling near Wilson's place, which is six miles above the Windmill ranch on the east side of the Verde.

Though a hundred or more mummified dwarfs have been found in the cliff dwellings along the Verde and Beaver creek, this is the first that has not had a full complement of fingers, toes and teeth. It is believed that he was a freak.

The mummy discovered by Wilson and Mrs. Smith was wrapped in coarse cotton cloth and had cotton which still contained seeds. It was determined long ago by scientists that the prehistoric races which inhabited this region grew cotton and wove cloth.

The right foot had been broken off and it has not yet been located. A number of other human bones are in the same cave and the missing foot may be among them.

Those who have examined the mummy, which is now at Wilson's farm, declare that the teeth are well formed and evidently those of an adult, thus disposing of the theory that the mummy may be the remains of an infant. The head is well formed and it is believed that the owner was not a person of defective mentality, regardless of his stature and shortage of digits.

THE SAN PEDRO MOUNTAINS MUMMY,
WHICH IS SIMILAR TO THE DUENDES OF
NEW MEXICO AND ARIZONA.

UNUSUAL MUMMY FOUND

Race of Dwarfs Believed to Have Once Inhabited Part of This Country.

An unusual mummy, only thirty-two inches long and believed to have belonged to a race of dwarfs, has been discovered in a cliff dwelling near Wilson's ranch on the east side of the Verde, according to a report received at Los Angeles, Cal., from Jerome, Ariz.

The pygmy has only twenty teeth, three fingers and a thumb on one hand, and four toes on the left foot. The right foot is missing.

The shortage of teeth, fingers and toes appear to have been natural with the individual, though hardly a racial trait, because at least one hundred mummies have been found in the cliff and cave dwellers along the Verde and on Beaver Creek, and this is the first one found not naturally constituted. The teeth and head are perfectly formed and undoubtedly belonged to an adult and not a child.

THIS PAGE AND FOLLOWING: VARIATIONS OF THE SAME ARTICLE.

A PREHISTORIC MUMMY.

Prospectors Make Some Interesting Discoveries.

Monday a party of prospectors on their way from Phoenix to Mangus, Colorado, stopped in town for a few hours. On their way here they spent a week at Montezuma Wells and at Montezuma's Castle, on Beaver creek. At the latter place there are a large number of prehistoric cliff dwellings, which the party investigated. They found the former burying ground of the extinct race and unearthed twenty skeletons. They were fortunate enough to find one mummified body, the first one, it is believed, that has been found, and they propose to take the mummy to Denver, where they expect to sell it.

Dr. D. J. Brannen was given an opportunity to examine the mummy and describes it as being a fine specimen and well preserved. The mummy is that of an adult male and of a pigmy race. It measured three and one-half feet in length. Of the skeletons found by the party none of them exceeded that height, which seems to have been the greatest stature obtained by the unknown race of people that once inhabited all this portion of Arizona.

It is unfortunate that the mummy could not be purchased from the travelers, as it should be in the possession of some one of our historical societies, and should remain in the Territory, instead of some Eastern museum.

On each hand are three perfectly formed fingers, opposed to a thumb which is extraordinary in no way whatever.

THE UNITED VERDE MINE.

Years ago a government archaeologist found over 30 tiny mummies in a cliff dwelling near Montezuma's castle. All of those had normally formed hands and feet but information as to the number of their teeth is lacking. In height they ranged from 18 to 36 inches. These mummies are now in the Smithsonian Institution at Washington. D.C. Some others were disinterred near the mouth of Oak creek but their bones were simply thrown upon the ground and are still to be found there.

For a long time the theory that the aborigines of this section mummified their dead children was generally held but many competent investigators finally reached the conclusion that at one time there were a race of dwarfs in the Verde country.

MONTEZUMA CASTLE.

Every cave in which the mummies have been found bears evidence of having been fired and many believe that the dwarfs were exterminated by the ancestors of the Indians that were here when the white man came.

COWBOYS & ZOMBIES

A different article specified that the finder of the mummies twenty years ago was John Love. While I could find no mentions of Love finding the mummies, I did find many mentions of him in Flagstaff from the time period at least. I did find earlier articles from about twenty years before that seem to be what the article was referring to. One, which amounted to only a small blurb, under "Territorial News" in the *Bisbee Cochise Review* of December 22, 1900, mentioned the finding of an Aztec mummy in the United Verde mine. Oddly, some tried to claim, or perhaps just jest, that it was the mummy of Emperor Montezuma himself.

The Jerome News gives an extended account of the alleged finding of a mummy in the United Verde mine. The finding of a mummy is a possible thing, but this alleged discovery coming on the heels of the finding of the bogus petrified man will make the story to be received with a large decoction of salt. After giving a very plausible account of the discovery the News spoils the story by claiming it to be that of Montezuma, the Aztec chief.

The find from twenty years ago may have been one that occurred in 1896, which was published in the *Flagstaff Coconino Weekly Sun* of March 19, 1896, on the front page:

A PREHISTORIC MUMMY.

Prospectors Make Some Interesting
Discoveries

COWBOYS & ZOMBIES

Monday a party of prospectors on their way from Phoenix to Mangus, Colorado, stopped in town for a few hours. On their way here they spent a week at Montezuma Wells and at Montezuma's Castle, on Beaver creek. At the later place there are a large number of prehistoric cliff dwellings, which the party investigated. They found the former burying ground of the extinct race and unearthed twenty skeletons. They were fortunate enough to find one mummified body, the first one, it is believed, that has been found, and they propose to lake the mummy to Denver, where they expect to sell it.

Dr. D. J. Branneu was given an opportunity to examine the mummy and describes it as being a fine specimen and well preserved. The mummy is that of an adult male and of a pigmy race. It measured three and one half feet in length. Of the skeletons found by the party none of them exceeded that height, which seems to have been the greatest stature obtained by the unknown race of people that once inhabited all this portion of Arizona.

It is unfortunate that the mummy could not be purchased from the travelers, as it should be in the possession of some one of our historical societies, and should remain in territory instead of some Eastern museum.

With this evidence in mind, and considering that the Southwest is rife with tales of duendes from both the Native Americans and Spanish settlers, perhaps there really was a race of mischievous Little People hiding in the Southwest? As stated before, there are still those who claim to see them to this day.

DUENDOCITOS **BY FRANCISCO GOYA, 1799.**

COWBOYS & ZOMBIES

Sources:

Espinosa, Aurelio M. "New-Mexican Spanish Folk-Lore." *The Journal of American Folklore* Vol. 23, No. 90 (Oct. - Dec., 1910).

Robinson, Sherry. *Apache Voices: Their Stories of Survival as Told to Eve Ball.* University of New Mexico Press, 2000.

JOHN LEMAY

ILLUSTRATION FROM THE
ALBUQUERQUE JOURNAL OF OCTOBER 24, 1978.

CHAPTER 5
LA LLORONA
AS A
ZOMBIE

LA LLORONA IS A GHOST; no doubt about it. But a few of her witnesses have affixed zombie-like attributes to her, so it would it be a shame not to give her a spot in the book. Also known as the Wailing Woman, La Llorona is essentially a Hispanic version of the Woman in White. Usually, but not always, she's associated with water, and oftentimes has drowned her children in an act of despair-induced insanity. After committing the horrible depredation, like a zombie, she shuffles along the waterways, wailing and crying as she searches out her dead children for eternity. And, in the process, she often takes children from the realm of the living to the land of the dead. In a few very rare cases, she's even been accused of eating children or drinking their blood in vampiric fashion.

Rather than a singular ghost, La Llorona is more so a *type* of ghost, as nearly every town or village in the Southwest has their own version of her that originated there.[29] In Mexico City, in particular, she is quite zombie-like in the sense that she appears as a skeleton woman.

CALAVERA CATRINA

There she would be seen walking calmly and quietly through the streets rather than running and shrieking. She would be wearing a white petticoat with a white rebozo covering her head. In his book, *Legends of the City of Mexico*, Thomas Janvier related:

---

[29] As to her true, historical origin, most will attribute that to the mistress of Hernán Cortés, La Malinche, spurned by the conquistador when he abandoned her and their two children to return to Spain without her. According to unsubstantiated folklore, Malinche then killed the children with a ritual dagger and then threw their bodies into Lake Texcoco in current-day Mexico City.

Meeting a watchman or a lonely traveler, she would cry out for her children, then disappear. He would lose consciousness or go mad. An officer who coaxed her to cast aside her rebozo was rewarded by the sight of a skeleton; he felt "an icy breath" and fell, unconscious. Later, having reported the incident, he died. To hear her is frightening; to see, to stop, to speak to her is very dangerous.[30]

ADVERTISEMENT FOR 1960's *LA LLORONA* FEATURE FILM FROM MEXICO.

J. Frank Dobie depicted La Llorona in a flesh-seeking manner, claiming that she was able to sniff out a corpse buried deep in the ground. Dobie also wrote that "Where men are hanged La Llorona comes, and one near such a place can feel her

---

[30] Janvier, *Legends of the City of Mexico*, pp.134-138.

breath as she passes. At any place where bandits bury a dead man to guard treasure she appears also."[31]

STILL FROM *LA LLORONA* (1930).

Las Vegas, New Mexico, has a bevy of different La Lloronas, all fixated on Bridge Street leading to the Gallinas River. One had nothing to do with dead children, and was decidedly zombie-like. "It is said that in the late 1800s, a woman's head was found in the middle of Bridge Street and no body was found to go with the head. The head was buried alone," related an old folkloric account from *Hispanic Legends from New Mexico.* The story continued, "Every spring, between twelve and one o'clock a woman's body without a head is seen and heard in Las Vegas. [The informant] has heard

---

[31] Dobie, *Tongues of the Monte*, p.78.

the cries of the woman. She has been named the llorona or 'cry woman.' It is said that she is looking for her head."[32] Another Las Vegas La Llorona tale had her as a skeletal woman in a veil picked up by a driver of the Lucero Taxi company. In that case, the skeletal woman jumped out of the cab while it traveled over the bridge.

In Arizona, a zombie-like La Llorona roams the outskirts of Tucson in search of human flesh. Her goal isn't to eat people, however, but to chop up their remains to reconstruct the bodies of her children, which were hacked to pieces by an abusive husband during the days of the Wild West. Per an informant to the *Tucson Citizen* named David Huet, for years, a series of unsolved grisly murders had plagued the Santa Cruz River, with various human remains in the form of severed limbs and headless bodies found in the vicinity.

There were so many that the Tucson Police Department kept a secret file on the murders. "There is, [Huet] says, locked away at the Tucson Police Department, a very old and very secret file. No one, save the very top law enforcement officials, may read it, for it contains the case reports dealing with the many mysterious bodies that have been found over the years," the *Tucson Citizen* reported. Of the unsolved murders, area residents knew the real culprit was the ghost, La Llorona, though.[33]

---

[32] Robe, *Hispanic Legends from New Mexico*, p.98.
[33] Schellie, "One night," *Tucson Citizen* (January 14, 1980).

In Castroville, east of San Antonio, Texas, La Llorona began her wandering and wailing before she died. In that case, she threw her two children into the river and for two years, wearing all white, she wandered up and down the river looking for the spot where she drowned her children in a trance-like state. During her two-year odyssey, the woman was said to have searched nearly every river in Texas until, finally, on the two-year anniversary of the murder, she found the spot along the Medina River where her children drowned. The woman then jumped from the same cliff she threw her children from to join them in death.

DOLORES RIVER DEPICTED ON POSTCARD.

The most zombie-like La Llorona of all is surely the one who drowned her children in Colorado's Dolores River. A fisherman supposedly saw a crying woman standing along the river's edge one night. When he reached out with a helping hand, the woman turned to face him. In her vacant eye sockets were squirming worms, mud clung to her black hair, and her head was bloated as though it had been submerged under water for some time. The woman let out a wicked laugh which sent the fisherman running to tell his tale.

So, again, though a ghost, La Llorona has a few zombie-like traits, especially when she appears as a decomposing corpse or a skeleton woman.

Sources:
Dobie, J. Frank. *Tongues of the Monte: The Mexico I Like.* Hammond, Hammond & Co., Ltd., 1948.

Janvier, Thomas A. *Legends of the City of Mexico.* Kindle Edition, 2017.

Robe, Stanley L. *Hispanic Legends from New Mexico (Folklore and Mythology Studies: 31).* University of California Press, 1980.

Schellie, Don. "One night you may hear La Llorona's Ghostly Wail." *Tucson Citizen.* (January 14, 1980).

Waters, Stephanie. *Colorado Legends & Lore: The Phantom Fiddler, Snow Snakes and Other Tales.* The History Press, 2014.

DEPICTION OF THE DWAYO, A
WEREWOLF-LIKE CREATURE THAT
SUCCEEDED THE SNARLY YOW AND
WHICH WAS SEEN IN THE MID-1960s.

CHAPTER 6
SNARLY YOW
WEST VIRGINIA WEREWOLF

KNOWN AS A HELLHOUND to some and a werewolf to others is the Snarly Yow. It entered folklore in the mid-1800s, though sightings extended further back into the previous century. The creature was often described as a large black dog notorious for its snarl—hence the name. The beast was mostly quadrupedal, though a few bipedal sightings also made it eligible to be a werewolf. Whatever it was, it haunted Maryland, Virginia, and West Virginia, with the highest concentration of sightings along the National Highway and the South Mountain region on the West Virginia Border. Many sightings of the creature were ghostly, with it vanishing either into thin air or into the Appalachian mists. Most tales told of it keeping pace with horse-drawn carriages, no matter how quickly the travelers tried to outpace it.

SOME THINK THE SNARLY YOW MAY BE LINKED TO THE BLOODY BATTLE OF SOUTH MOUNTAIN ON SEPTEMBER 14, 1862.

Most typical sightings described the dog-like creature as being larger than a normal canine, black-furred, and with either red eyes or a red mouth, if not both.[34] The paws were also said to be larger than normal.[35] Sightings peaked in the early 1900s and dwindled off until another prominent encounter occurred in the mid-1970s—hence my speaking of it in the past tense.

And just how well-known was the Snarly Yow? It ranked highly enough in state folklore for a historical marker in Boonsboro, Maryland, to be

---

[34] On a few occasions the eyes were yellow rather than red.

[35] Other alterations, according to George Dudding in *The Snarly Yow*, included the creature as a white dog dragging a chain and also as a headless dog.

erected. According to the story on the marker, a South Mountain hunter took a shot at the Snarly Yow only to watch as his bullet sailed straight through the beast as though it were simply an illusion. Ultimately, it was one of many similar accounts.

Some have speculated that the creature had something to do with the bloody battles of the Civil War, but accounts of the beast actually dated back to German settlers who arrived in the 1700s.[36] Among those settlers was an alleged "wizard" named Michael Zittle, who moved to the area with his family during the time. Whether he was truly a wizard or not is folkloric, but he certainly did exist.[37] Author George Dudding even speculated that perhaps this wizard somehow manifested the Snarly Yow into existence to patrol the mountain where he lived. Specifically, it was thought the Snarly Yow was created to protect the spring that the Zittles used. An old 1882 book entitled *South Mountain Magic* seemed to confirm this: "...others, again, suppose it to be some animal who stalks from its lair at night to slake its thirst at the wayside spring, where it has been asserted that it was seen."[38] The same author also noted how the beast seemed to "guard the pass," so perhaps it was linked to the Zittles. Considering that Zittle arrived

---

[36] These same settlers also brought with them tales of the Snallygaster.

[37] A monument to their existence remains in the form of the ruins of the village of Zittlestown, very near Glendale where the Snarly Yow was often seen.

[38] Dahlgren, *South Mountain Magic*, p.76.

in the area at the same time that the Snarly Yow began appearing, it's no wonder why people connected the wizard with the werewolf.

It also didn't hurt that the beast's main haunt lies along a ley line. Ley Lines are similar to Window Areas and consist of straight alignments on a map that stretch between ancient landmarks of significance and modern structures as well. The idea was that the ancients deliberately built structures along these lines. Along the Snarly Yow's ley line is the Washington Monument (not to be confused with the one in Washington D.C., this one was constructed in Boonsboro in 1827). Author Dudding again supposed that perhaps Zittle used the stone monument in rituals.

In any case, much of what we know of the Snarly Yow came from author Madeleine Vinton Dahlgren, who purchased the South Mountain Inn in Maryland in 1876. The widow soon became fascinated with local area lore, resulting in her book *South Mountain Magic,* quoted previously. A creature that she heard locals refer to as the Dog Fiend especially intrigued her because, even though it was obviously supernatural, the locals didn't question its existence. To them it was as real as a rattlesnake. Notably, several times in the book, Dahlgren referred to the Dog Fiend/Snarly Yow as a werewolf. Since it is usually best to go with sources closest to the time period, we will quote from her book heavily. Specifically, of its general appearance, Dahlgren wrote that the "Snarly Yow and the Were-Wolf" were said to "guard the pass." As did many others, she described it as a black dog "of a mystic shining; now waning, now increasing, it crosses the ravine, or disappears like a light suddenly blown out."[39]

Dahlgren went on to note that the apparition was often sighted in the same locale, and she rationally argued that "The different accounts all agree in the main points, and are difficult to dispose of by a mere denial, or by the charge of hallucination, which may more readily perhaps be made than sustained."[40]

However, Dahlgren also noted that, "If indeed such an animal ranged the forest, it would at least occasionally commit depredations." Or, in other words, unlike a real wolf or wild canine, the Snarly Yow was never known to kill animals—or, at least, no corpses thought to have been the result of the Snarly Yow were reported. Notably, Dahlgren collected firsthand witness accounts of the beast, though she often concealed the witnesses' identities, as evidenced in this passage from pages 79-80:

Our first narrator, and a credible witness, is William L----e. He is a good type of a sturdy mountain man. A sober, laborious, strong, and trustworthy young man, of perhaps thirty years of age. He is married, and lives with his little family in the first cabin on the brow of the hill that overlooks Glendale. His hut is not over a quarter of a mile from the alleged habitat of the Black Dog.

---

[39] Ibid, p.72.
[40] Ibid, p.73.

One night about ten o'clock, as he was returning from the village of Boonsboro, whither he had gone to make some little purchases for his family, he encountered the Black Dog.

It was clear starlight, and the ungainly form of the beast could be distinctly traced. It was black, and bigger than any dog he had ever seen; and, as he came nearer, the object intercepted him, and stood guarding the road in such a way as to forbid his crossing. So, to use his own expression, he "*fit him.*" That is, nothing daunted, he fought at him. But, to his confusion, as the creature was attacked, it "grew longer," and presently seemed to extend across the road, making no noise, but showing a very wide and very ugly-looking red mouth; while, all the time the thick and heavy blows rained down upon it, the sinewy arm of the woodsman met with no resistance, but rather seemed to beat the air.

Presently the still lengthening shadow passed onward, and then the man, not a little flurried at the strange nature of the vision, went home; — nor did he receive the least bodily harm from this ominous combat.

But we have several times heard him tell this story when questioned about it, and when one looks upon the erect and well-knit figure of this "stalwart tiller of the soil," and his firm and composed bearing, one cannot but wonder how such a man could have had a spectral illusion.

Next, Dahlgren offered the testimony of an unnamed farmer who asserted that as he was passing along the gorge one night, he sighted the Snarly Yow. As he did so, he said that he felt like "the hill was coming down upon him"[41] and he nearly became paralyzed with fear. Another unnamed witness claimed that at the sight of the dog, they were "seized with a sort of 'color blindness,' as the vision assumed various hues, at times 'coal black,' then again changing into great spots of white."[42] An itinerant preacher claimed to see it on three different occasions, all of which occurred after holding evening prayer-meetings in a church near Glendale. Dahlgren also gave the full account of the hunter used on the marker:

> Mr. W--y, who is considered "a sure shot," relates to have met it crossing the road. He carried his ever-ready rifle with him, and feeling sure of his aim, shot at it with steady hand when within a few paces. To his speechless amazement, the well-directed shot went right through the animal without effect. Again and again the sharp crack of the trusted rifle was heard, as it was sent with deadly accuracy, and went whizzing through and through the shadow, leaving no mark. Overcome with dread at the uncanny sight, the huntsman fled, nor stopped to see if the shade retreated or pursued.[43]

---

[41] Ibid, pp.80-81.
[42] Ibid, p.81.
[43] Ibid, pp.81-82.

Beware of the "Snarly Yow"

Legend has it that the shadow of a black dog used to prowl the heights of South Mountain. One night, a huntsman, famous as a sure shot, encountered the beast. He aimed and fired his rifle. The shot went right through the animal with no effect. He fired again and again, each shot passing through the shadowy beast. Finally, overcome with dread, the huntsman fled.

THE HISTORICAL MARKER.

Another of the more interesting pioneer accounts of the Snarly Yow collected by Dahlgren had a local character named Big Joe chasing the ghost dog on horseback until it vanished into thin air. (This was a rare case of a person chasing the Snarly Yow as opposed to it chasing them.) Another popular story had a ruffian causing trouble at a local celebration, resulting in his expulsion. As the man fled the police on horseback, the Snarly Yow appeared before his horse, causing it to buck the man off, breaking his collarbone in the process.

COWBOYS & ZOMBIES

The Snarly Yow is said to be "a spook of very awful mien and huge proportions," in the guise of a waggoner," according to Mrs Dahlgren.

The Snarly Yow would guard a pass at South Mountain by rising out of the depths of the earth in the dark of night.

Besides the Snarly Yow, which reportedly hurt no one, but frightened many, the Dog Fiend or Black Dog was also a menace in days gone by.

The Dog Fiend roamed over the South Mountain area, Mrs. Dahlgren said in her book, and was described as being black, and bigger than my other animal with a wide, red mouth

South Mountain was apparently a hang - out in those days for all types of beasts and spooks, including the Phantom Soldier which just sat along a small stream, as did the Soldier Spook.

Besides these unknown monsters, everyday type creatures such as the headless man, a Were-Wolf and the White Woman, also were found in the Frederick - Washington county area at South Mountain.

SNIPPET FROM AN ARTICLE ON THE SNARLY YOW FROM THE *FREDERICK NEWS POST* OF DECEMBER 16, 1965.

While all of these accounts were predominantly of the ghostly dog variety, Dahlgren did dig up at least one classic werewolf-type sighting, full moon and all:

The wife of a farmer who lives on the summit beyond South-Mountain-House, and who is a woman of physical strength and nerve, as well as of very good judgment and what is called common sense, told us that, coming up the gorge one night with her husband in a sleigh, the moon being well up and the night bright, she distinctly saw the animal standing near the spring; that it was of much larger size than any dog she had ever seen, but looked, as it stood against the snowy bank, brown in color; that, as they approached it, the horse snorted, and was so restive as to demand all her husband's attention, and that she was afraid to point it out to him, as she knew, from his fearless character, that he would insist upon stopping to attack it. As they passed on, with the instinct that women have inherited from Lot's wife, she looked back, and there it stood, just as she had first seen it.[44]

For the most part, sightings of the beast began to dwindle when automobiles started replacing the horse and carriage. However, history repeated itself as the terrifying black dog returned in the 1970s, keeping pace with cars as their drivers watched in terror just like the pioneers of yore. The

---

[44] Ibid, p.84.

best-known Snarly Yowl encounter of this era occurred in 1975. Supposedly, a man hit the spectral canine with his car when it appeared in front of him. However, though he knew he had to have hit the dog as it never moved out of the way, he never felt an impact. Confused, he still pulled over to check for damage. There was no damage, nor was there a dead dog. Suddenly, he heard a low growling behind him and turned to see a demonic dog with glowing red eyes. The animal began to grow via strange supernatural means, and so the man hopped back into his car and sped away with the monstrous canine on his tail. Like all ghosts, the specter simply disappeared after the man drove off.

A better alternative to that story was presented in Dave Spink's *The West Virginia Dogman*, and stated instead that the witness, here named George, stopped his car rather than hitting the creature. George exited his vehicle and began casting stones at the large dog in hopes that it would get off the road. But like the South Mountain hunter, the stones simply passed through the ghostly canine. The Snarly Yow growled at the man, but then decided to simply saunter off into the woods and leave the man in peace. This encounter was said to have occurred in the area of Glendale.

As it stands, this was the last major sighting of the Snarly Yow, and since then it has stuck to the recesses of folklore.

Sources:

Dahlgren, Madeleine Vinton. *South Mountain Magic: Tales of Old Maryland.* Lethe Press, 2002.

Dudding, George. *The Snarly Yow.* Independently published, 2020.

Fair, Susan. *Mysteries and Lore of Western Maryland: Snallygasters, Dogmen and other Mountain Tales.* The History Press, 2013.

Spinks, Dave. *The West Virginia Dogman.* Independently published, 2022.

THE ZOMBIE OF CRIPPLE CREEK.

The mining hub that is Cripple Creek, Colorado, took off around 1874 when a prospector named Crazy Bob Womack struck gold in the ironically named Poverty Gulch. As gold-mining boomtowns were wont to do, it soon became a hub of sin and depravity, and the gunfighters and outlaws supplied a steady stream of corpses for the undertakers at Lampman and Black Funeral Parlor, where one of the dead notoriously revived. Per the *Cripple Creek Morning Times* of October 15, 1898, which screamed the headline "CAME BACK TO LIFE," apparently, a mangled prospector, thought dead, had set back up in his coffin and attempted to speak. Per the paper:

> If I live to be 1000 years, I would never again expect to see such an awful sight. There sat that THING actually sitting up in the coffin with bloody eyelashes, face, grinning teeth and hanging jaw, ogling and moving uncertainly about... It had worked with the stumps of its arms until the coffin lid had given away and fallen off. The noise had brought the attendant who had been sleeping in the office and he simply collapsed at the sight. I walked over to where the THING was swaying about in the coffin and it actually tried to speak but its broken jaw, torn tongue and throat made it unintelligible. It lived until early morning and then died.

Although this was most likely just the case of a poor man thought to be dead being buried prematurely, his ghost, still referred to as "The Thing," haunted the funeral parlor for many years to come. It was said that afterward, the funeral directors began sprinkling the hallways with holy water and hung crucifixes in every room. They also indulged in the old-time custom of turning their clothing inside out as a way of preventing possession by "The Thing."

Sources:

Waters, Stephanie. *Colorado Legends & Lore: The Phantom Fiddler, Snow Snakes and Other Tales.* The History Press, 2014.

CHAPTER 7
HEX CAT DODGES BULLET OF GOLD

WITCHES HAVE ALWAYS been associated with black cats. For instance, according to folklore, black cats were said to possess an invisible bone connected to the dark forces. A witch would boil a black cat in her cauldron until nothing remained but the bones. Then, she would inspect the bones one by one in a mirror. Whichever bone cast no reflection, much like a vampire, was the special "invisible" bone. Though no invisible bones came into play, what follows is still surely the black cat story to end all black cat stories.

It all started in September of 1911, when the Thomas family of Tumbling Run, a valley in rural Pennsylvania, began experiencing a run of very bad luck, the worst of which was the death of the patriarch, Howell Thomas. As such, it would be the survivors comprising his two daughters, the spinster Mary Thomas and the married Sarah Potts, that formed the backbone of the story. Also in the mix was their uncle, William Thomas, who would play a prominent role in the tale, too.

DEPICTION OF HEX CAT IN THE *POTTSVILLE REPUBLICAN* OF SEPTEMBER 30, 1911.

As it was, Howell Thomas's death was preceded by the arrival of a peculiar black cat seen around the farm in the early morning hours. Black cats had typically been considered bad omens, but this one was something special. After it began its nightly prowls, strange phenomena occurred, such as hens crowing like roosters, pigs barking like dogs, and livestock becoming sick and dying. Under the circumstances, the feline was dubbed the Hex Cat.

HEX CAT DODGES BULLET OF GOLD

Feline Blamed For Casting Spell Over Family.

PEOPLE STIRRED BY STORY

While "Hex" Tales From Tumbling
Run Have Created Derision, the Au
thorities Are Surprised at Number
of Weird Complaints.

RECORD-HERALD **OF SEPTEMBER 28, 1911.**

Prior to the Hex Cat's arrival, a fortune teller had warned the family to be weary of relatives from Orwigsburg out to get them. So, when the feline appeared and the bad luck began, they believed the Hex Cat was a result of their relatives' dark magic. However, as the story developed, these shadowy relatives faded into the background, and Mary Thomas began blaming her sister, Sarah Potts, for the Hex Cat. Mary, who had allied herself with Uncle William, believed that perhaps it was Sarah who was using the Hex Cat to get the family farm.

One night, Mary sat outside in wait for the cat with a rifle. When she shot the Hex Cat, the bullet appeared to sail right through it, and the cat grew to be four feet long before disappearing again. This all but confirmed her suspicions that the cat was truly bewitched, and so she consorted with various mediums on how to kill it. One suggested a golden bullet—which may or may not have killed the cat, more on that later—and another suggested a special black cat to fight it to the death. Adding to the confusion, another article claimed the Hex Cat was captured and put on display.

To this day, it's uncertain what happened to the Hex Cat, if it even existed at all. But one thing was certain, the papers had a field day with the story. In the best sequence that can be reconstructed, the most pertinent articles to chronicle the Hex Cat and its reign of terror will be reprinted, beginning with the *Record-Herald* of September 28, 1911, which picked up the story with Mary Thomas's first attempt to kill the cat with the golden bullet:

HEX CAT DODGES BULLETS OF GOLD

Pottsville, Pa., Sept. 28.—In the gray of the early morning a score of the more intrepid farmers of Tumbling Run Valley and a few interested ones, on invitations given by Miss Mary Isabella Thomas, who alleges that a "hex" or witch has placed a spell on the family through the machinations of a relative living in Orwigsburg, watched in vain for the appearance at the farm house of the black cat, which the young woman says has assumed gigantic shape, at times reaching the maximum height of four feet. They waited with a gun loaded with a gold bullet, but the feline for the first time in many weeks failed to put in an appearance.

Spirit Frightened Away

Some of her waiting guests believe the evil spirit was frightened away by reason of the fact that they carried Bibles, crucifixes and talismans to break witches' spells. Miss Thomas says that the big cat will surely appear some morning, and then either she or her uncle will shoot it with the golden bullet. They have great faith in the precious metal messenger of death, although lead bullets failed them on other occasions. Miss Thomas has taken up her residence with a neighbor, and the haunted farmhouse has been deserted.

Since she made public her statements that a "hex" is following the family, she has had five offers of marriage. She has decided to accept none of them. Mrs. Sarah Potts has offered to give her sister, Mary, a home with her, despite the fact that she is named by the latter as being the author of the family's misfortunes. Miss Thomas still possesses charms sent to her by a California witch doctor, and she says that she will guard them closely for future use.

Farmers Wrought Up

The farmers of the Tumbling Run Valley are greatly wrought up over this mysterious "hex" case and want the strange affair thoroughly sifted to the bottom. The Republican, of Pottsville, the largest daily, in an editorial asks for an investigation.

While the "hex" stories from Tumbling Run have created derision and laughter in Pottsville, the authorities were surprised at the number of weird complaints which came in from that vicinity. One farmer, who has brought a large quantity of milk from the Tumbling Run Valley for many years, declares that the fresh fluid was discolored as he brought it to market. There were also three automobile accidents in that vicinity.

The saga continued in the story headlined "Called Sister a Witch" printed in various papers, but this one came from *The Inquirer* of September 30, 1911. Notably, it implied the Hex Cat was killed by the golden bullet in the headline, though the article itself seemed to contradict that. It also added a new flourish to the story, that of sulfur fumes stinking up the farm and Mary Thomas becoming ill.

CALLED SISTER WITCH.
Says Her Own Kin "Cast a Spell"
Over the Family and Caused
Very Many Troubles.
THE FAMILY BELIEVE IN THE "HEX"
Used a Golden Bullet to Kill a Cat
That Is Believed to Be the Demon
That Took Death to the House.

CALLED SISTER WITCH.

Says Her Own Kin "Cast a Spell"
Over the Family and Caused
Very Many Troubles.

ALL THE FAMILY BELIEVE IN THE "HEX"

Used a Golden Bullet to Kill a Cat
That Is Believed to Be the Demon
That Took Death to
the House.

Miss Mary Isabella Thomas, who says her father, Howell Thomas, was killed by a "hex," or witch, spell, created a scene at the funeral of Mr. Thomas, near Pottsville, on Tuesday, when she accused her sister, Mrs. Sarah Potts, of "casting the spell."

Miss Thomas, over her father's coffin, ordered her sister out of the room where the services were held. After the services Miss Thomas again confronted her sister and in the excitement fainted. Mrs. Potts was almost overcome.

Miss Mary Isabella Thomas, who says her father, Howell Thomas, was killed by a "hex," or witch, spell, created a scene at the funeral of Mr. Thomas, near Pottsville, on Tuesday, when she accused her sister, Mrs. Sarah Potts, of "casting the spell."

Miss Thomas, over her father's coffin, ordered her sister out of the room where the services were held. After the services Miss Thomas again confronted her sister and in the excitement fainted. Mrs. Potts was almost overcome.

The queer beliefs of Miss Thomas and some of her relatives have kept this community stirred since Mr. Thomas died last week. There was more excitement before dawn next morning, when the "witch cat," which the Thomases declared to be the medium by which the "hex" was conveyed to the Thomas homestead, was killed. Miss Thomas used gold bullets to kill the cat, this being the advice of a witch doctor.

Not only is the death of Howell Thomas charged to the "hex," but also a long series of misfortunes at the Thomas homestead, in Tumbling Run valley. These include the pining away of horses, cattle and poultry, the illness of Miss Thomas and strange appearance of sulphur fumes, one of the witch-demon's annoyances.

At the deathbed request of Howell Thomas, his funeral was held in Pottsville. Mary Isabella Thomas, the unmarried daughter, had previously accused a family in Orwigsburg of placing the "hex" on her father, but it was not known until Tuesday that she blamed her sister. Miss Thomas announced that she would not let Mrs. Potts attend the funeral.

Many persons thereabouts believe in the "hex," and there was a throng at the house where services were held. Several minutes before the time set for the ceremony, Mrs. Potts, her husband and their three children drove up to the house. Miss Thomas became very much excited and refused to permit the sister to enter. Standing by the coffin, she accused the married sister with being responsible for the death of her father, and for a time there was much excitement. Friends finally quieted Miss Thomas and, after Mrs. Potts had retired, leaving the three children in the room, the services were held.

Miss Thomas, who was in a highly nervous state, was induced to go upstairs and while there Mrs. Potts reentered the house. Miss Thomas broke away from the women who attempted to restrain her and rushed downstairs and again ordered her married sister out of the house. She then fell in a faint. With the aid of smelling salts she was revived and was able to go to the cemetery. Mrs. Potts also went to the cemetery.

While Mrs. Potts was at the coffin she dropped over on the floor several times, weeping. She exclaimed: "My God! My God; father, I did not know I was accused of anything until I saw it in the papers. And they wouldn't let me see you while you were alive."

"Yes," said the unmarried sister, "he saw you all the time."

After the funeral, Miss Thomas went among her neighbors, farmers residing in the Tumbling Run valley, and requested them to come to the Thomas farm next morning at 3:45 o'clock to witness the killing of the "witch cat." Although she says it had been shot at frequently, the bullets did not take effect because they were made of lead. She says a witch doctor told her to melt $5 gold pieces and make bullets, as these were the only kind to kill the beast.

Daniel Howell, a brother of the dead man, said in an interview that his niece was taken suddenly ill some time ago, and it was a question whether she would ever recover. Two prominent physicians were called in to attend her, this "hex" believer says, and, although they did everything in their power, the girl grew weaker and weaker. This continued for nearly eight weeks, when, according to the uncle, the first part of a "spell" placed upon the girl was broken and she started to regain her health. The uncle believes the "spell" is still on the family.

"The demon has evidently determined to get the remainder of the family, and in this he may succeed," said the uncle. "For the past two days my niece has been in Pottsville, and everywhere she has walked she has been followed by this unseen spirit."

Howell told how it was possible to shut every window and door in the Thomas house, to stop up every crack where it was likely that air would enter, and then, all of a sudden, to be thrown to the floor as the result of sulphur fumes. A stranger, he said, could be seated in the house and alongside members of the family; with the house all closed tight. Suddenly, he declared, the sulphur would come, knock down the member of the family, while the person sitting close by would never detect the odor; or it could work the other way, the stranger being knocked down and the family not notice the fumes. This has repeatedly occurred at the homestead in the Tumbling Run valley, he said.

"Hex" is simply the Pennsylvania name for witchcraft, belief in which has persisted in certain parts of this state since colonial times, despite the advance in science and in general education.

It was around this point that the story seriously became confused regarding the fate of the witch cat. The previous article even contradicted itself, claiming in the headline and early in the article that the Hex Cat was successfully dispatched via the golden bullet. However, later in the same article, it only spoke of Mary Thomas planning to kill the cat the night after her father's funeral. The papers continued to print contradictory stories, with the next round stating that the cat had been captured, like this one from the *Spokesman Review* of October 8, 1911:

Pottsville, Pa.--Captured by a Bible thrown at it, the only witch cat the "hex" believers of Schuylkill county known to be in captivity, has been exhibited in a show window here, behind eight-inch steel bars, where "hex" doctors are anxiously studying the creature to determine whether it is the animal which Miss Mary Thomas blames for the death of her father and a long train of other misfortunes in the Thomas family.

The cat was captured by Charles Lawless, one of the posse which had been looking for the demon creature described by Miss Thomas as sometimes taking on four-foot proportions during calls at the Thomas farm. Having failed to appear while men armed with a gold bullet lay in wait for it Lawless provided himself with an old blunderbuss, said to have been blessed by a saint, a web taken from the intestines of a pure white lamb, a book of counter action voices against witches' spells, and many other talismans, and was rewarded for his labors by the appearance of a black cat as he watched on the Thomas farm.

Too much excited to use his gun Thomas threw a Bible at the cat, whereupon it walked over to Lawless, spit in his face and clawed him. Lawless got a good grip on pussy, however, and brought her to town, though Miss Thomas wasn't sure that it was the witch cat. The cat has the witching green eyes. Lawless has been advised by several witch doctors from various parts of the country to guard the cat closely, some mystic words being supplied to keep it a close prisoner, until they can carefully inspect it and ascertain positively whether it is really a "hex" cat.

An article preceding that one gave a different account of the capture entirely and was printed by the *Pottsville Republican* a week before in their

September 30th edition. It stated that after its capture, the cat was displayed at the Gately & Brennan furniture store on West Market Street. The editor of the *Republican* went to see it for himself, and claimed that the cat seemed to be possessed of an evil spirit. If the editor really meant it or was just playing along is difficult to say.

The capture of the cat by Charles Lawless was very different from the rendition printed on October 7th. According to the editor of the *Republican,* Lawless was riding his horse and buggy through Tumbling Run when he heard what he thought was a child calling in distress.[45] He traced the noise to a hollowed-out tree trunk. Peering into the darkness, he saw two bright feline eyes glowing at him. Nothing was said of a Bible being thrown at the beast. Lawless ran to his buggy to get a large blanket, which he enveloped the cat in and then took it to the furniture store. The men swiftly and fearfully constructed a cage "that could hold an elephant" to secure the Hex Cat.

As was to be expected, once the cat was secured, strange things began happening along West Market Street. The editor claimed that when he went to the store, the horses acted oddly, refusing to eat, and even the phone lines seemed to be having issues. Somehow the cat even escaped the confines of the box and had to be recaptured. The editor described the Hex Cat thusly,

---

[45] This is a common method of many supernatural creatures from the skinwalker to the owl witch, Lechuza, I might add, which I find interesting.

JOHN LEMAY

"THE BLACK CAT"
BY LIONEL LINDSAY (1922).

The cat is as black as the ace of spades. It is about medium size and weighs two or three pounds with large yellow eyes, the size of a 25 cent piece, and tall, nearly two feet long, it presents a horrible sight. Its feet are nearly twice the size of an ordinary cat and when angry its back comes up in the air and it is then ready to make the fur fly.

COWBOYS & ZOMBIES

The editor saw the cat returned to the box, whereupon it made a second supernatural escape attempt:

To the observer it appeared as though its body became oblong or in other words grew to twice its normal length. The size of the head diminished until it appeared to be about three feet long and one inch in thickness. The cat then ran its tail up through the slats on the box and twisting it around the one slat started to pull itself up, the same as a monkey hanging by its tail.

When it was about halfway out, one of the men pushed the cat back in. The owners did not wish to keep the cat and intended to hire some brave soul to come along and shoot it with another golden bullet. Instead, there was a blackout that night and the cat escaped. It was later seen darting across a road, causing a horse and buggy to tip over, injuring the passengers in the process.

Efforts to kill the Hex Cat resumed in the *Black Hills Daily Register* of October 5, 1911:

Are After the "Hex" Cat.
Pottsville, Pa., Oct. 5.—The final chapter of the weird performances in Tumbling Run valley, where Fanner Howell Thomas, according to relatives, was killed by the evil charm of a "hex" cat, was enacted at a meeting of powwow doctors from Schuylkill Haven.

Ever since preparations were made to shoot the "hex" cat with a gold bullet, it has failed to put in an appearance at the Thomas farm, and the "hex" doctors decided that the evil spell cast over the Thomas homestead can only be dispelled by installing a certain other black cat, now owned by a Schuylkill Haven man.

This cat is said to have been born on the sixth day of the sixth month in 1906, and to have been one of a litter of six kittens. It was blind only six days after being born, whereas all ordinary cats are blind nine days.

The "hex" doctors declare that these facts make this a "hexahemeron" cat. According to powwow erudition, the word "hexahemeron" is taken from Greek words "hex" and "hemera," and means a completion in six parts. They refer probably to the word "hexamerous," the Greek origin. The word is usually used, they say, in referring to the six days' labor of creation, as described in the first chapter of Genesis. While there are only five books of Moses in the authorized bible, the "hex" doctors declare they have a sixth book of Moses. In this novel book the witch of Endor, who raised up Samuel and who is referred to in the bible as being consulted by Saul, ascribes full power to the hemamerous cat in warding off evil spells.

It was declared that the "hex" cat that vanished, had beyond doubt an engagement with the evil one, whereby it had imparted to it an imp or familiar spirit. The Schuylkill Haven cat has never eaten anything but toads, frogs, lizards and serpents, and the "hex" doctors agreed that its presence will restore the Thomas homestead to a normal condition. The assurance of relief seems to have already affected the Thomas farm, for the hundreds of visitors to the bewitched place found that the hens were no longer crowing like roosters nor were the pigs barking like dogs.

THE

SIXTH AND SEVENTH

BOOKS OF MOSES;

OR,

MOSES' MAGICAL SPIRIT-ART,

KNOWN AS THE

WONDERFUL ARTS

OF THE OLD WISE HEBREWS, TAKEN FROM THE MOSAIC BOOKS OF THE CABALA AND THE TALMUD, FOR THE GOOD OF MANKIND.

Translated from the German, Word for Word, according to Old Writings.

WITH NUMEROUS ENGRAVINGS.

New York:

1880.

THE SIXTH AND SEVENTH BOOKS OF MOSES MENTIONED IN THE ARTICLE.

Did the Hex Cat and the "Hexahemeron Cat" come to blows like King Kong and Godzilla? Did the Hex Cat meet its end like a werewolf, albeit with a golden bullet buried in its breast? If the newspapermen really were making up the story, then they dropped the ball on the conclusion. So far as anyone knows, the Hex Cat simply disappeared after its capture. (And with a lackluster ending like that, perhaps the story did have some basis in reality?) The closest thing to a real conclusion was printed in the *Allentown Democrat* of February 24, 1912, and was as follows:

FIND "HEX" CAT FROZEN
Hoodoo Supposed to Have Vanished
From Tumbling Run.

Joy again reigns in the Tumbling Run Valley, near Pottsville, the home of the famous "Hex" cat, because the farmers now declare that the uncanny machinations of the evil feline have at last been broken. There are many reasons assigned by the agriculturalists for believing that the evil spirit that brooded over the quiet valley and caused the death of William Thomas is gone. The most remarkable is that which has just transpired at the farm of Chirtsian [sic] Wagner, which is close by the Thomas farm, the seat of the "Hex" disturbances, until the temperature started to register 15 and 20 degrees below zero, which led to the report that the cat that awed the entire lower county had been frozen to death.

COWBOYS & ZOMBIES

Mr. Wagner was one of the farmers affected by misfortune until he purchased twin calves early last summer. There must have been favorable magic in the buying of the bovines, for they have brought him good luck ever since, both are now full grown cows, and this week, though on separate days, each of the cows gave birth to twin calves. This circumstance is remarkable enough; but the good fortune of Farmer Wagner has given rise to the belief that the spell of the "Hex" cat has gone, never to be felt again, in the Tumbling Run portion of Schuylkill county, at all events.

Miss Isabella Thomas, who was the author of the story of the strange doings of the black cat of evil fame, is now occupying the old homestead, and has declined to discuss the matter of her alleged "fer-Hexed" family, even with her close friends, another reason for believing that the supernatural presence has disappeared.

And yet, the saga of the Hex Cat still has what we could either call an epilogue or a mini-sequel. Remember Uncle William? According to the *Reading Eagle* of June 16, 1916, the Hex Cat was at it again five years later:

Pottsville, June 16.--William R. Thomas, who achieved wide notoriety three years ago by his allegations that the burning of his barn at his Tumbling Run farm and numerous deaths in his family, ending in the ruination of the farm, were due to the spell cast by a big black cat, was arrested by the police of this city while he was in the act of setting fire to a double tenement building owned by him on North Third street.

Thomas had soaked the two houses in oil and but for the timely discovery of his plot a dangerous fire in the heart of the city would have been started.

Since the "persecutions" of the hex cat, on the once prosperous Thomas farm, Thomas has lived in this city, but he lately declared the cat was again pursuing him.

He had $1,000 insurance on the building, but this would not pay a mortgage having the first claim. In the possession of Thomas was found a revolver in which was a silver bullet, molded by Thomas himself.

Thomas declared that lead bullets passed clear through the cat without harming it. Thomas' niece, Miss Alda Thomas, who also declares she has been bewitched by the hex cat, tried to shoot herself when taken into custody by the police.

There's a lot to unpack in that little article, firstly that in 1913 Thomas' barn burned down and he blamed it on the Hex Cat, sight unseen since 1911. The fact that he really was found with a silver bullet would seem to imply that newspaper reports of five years ago were not exaggerated, and the Thomas family really was convinced not only of the cat's existence, but of its supernatural power. Lastly, the mention of "Miss Alda Thomas," his niece, brings to mind Mary Thomas and one has to wonder if that's who the paper was really referring to. Perhaps they got her name wrong, or maybe she was by then using an alias.

As for William Thomas, he was sentenced to three months in jail. After serving his sentence, he was found frozen to death in a little shack in the Tumbling Run Valley in 1918.

AN ILLUSTRATION OF POTTSVILLE IN 1854.

Today, the Hex Cat incident is still remembered by area historians and is sometimes still used, albeit jokingly, as the cause of bad luck in the area. In retrospect, modern folklorists and historians agree that Howell Thomas simply died of a stroke, that the farm was in a deplorable state before the cat ever showed up, and that all the bad luck could be attributed to natural causes.

Leo Ward, president of the local historical society in 1995, also confirmed that there was no discernable conclusion to the saga of the Hex Cat. In his article, "'Hex Cat' On Prowl," in the *Republican and Herald* of October 21, 1995, he concluded, "Did the gold bullets kill the cat, or is it still roaming the Tumbling Run valley in search of an unsuspecting hex victim?"[46]

SATIRICAL DEPICTION OF THE HEX CAT FROM *THE POTTSVILLE REPUBLICAN* OF SEPTEMBER 30, 1911.

---

[46] Ward, "Hex Cat' On Prowl," *Republican and Herald* (October 21, 1995), p.18.

CHAPTER 8
HEADLESS HORSEMAN
OF THE
KIAMICHI MOUNTAINS

ONE OF THE MORE UNIQUE "zombies" of the Old West was another headless horseman, this one of the Choctaw Nation. The headless rider served as an omen to anyone who might try to disturb a treasure of minted U.S. gold coins. The treasure had a complicated history in that it was part of a $2 million settlement with the Choctaw Nation on behalf of the U.S. government, which had seized unallotted lands from them. The payment was made in 1858, with $250,000 worth of it being issued in gold coins. The rest was to be given in the form of bonds over the next several years. However, when the Choctaw sided with the Confederacy during the Civil War, the deal was rendered moot. Thus, all they had was the cache of gold coins, which the Choctaw Nation hid.

The gold was buried somewhere near the Kiamichi River in Oklahoma under the orders of George Hudson, principal chief of the Choctaw Nation at the time. He ordered the gold to be hidden because the Union Army was on the move, and he feared they might seize the gold coins. To do so, Hudson sent out two men of the tribe to secret the gold away, which they did by hiding it in a small cave near the river. Over the course of the war, several of the men who had hidden the coins died in the fighting, leaving Escar Colbert as the lone survivor by the time the war ended.

GEORGE HUDSON, PRINCIPAL CHIEF OF THE CHOCTAW NATION.

COWBOYS & ZOMBIES

Though a map to the treasure had been made by the Choctaw Council, during several swift and forced moves, it had been misplaced over the years. When Colbert returned from the war, badly mangled, he was unable to lead anyone back to the cave itself, and could only offer vague directions from a memory now clouded by the trauma of war. Worse yet, word of the treasure had spread, and the Kiamichi Mountains were already being scoured by outlaws on the hunt for it.

Colbert, having regained some strength, led an expedition in search of the cave again in 1867 with several other Choctaw men. After several days of scouring various caves, they finally found the right one... or so it seemed. In the dead of night, they descended the mountain on which the cave resided, carrying with them what appeared to be bags of gold. Unbeknownst to them, outlaws were watching. The men were former Quantrill raiders from Missouri. With their rifles at the ready, they began a swift and deadly massacre on the mountain. Colbert was atop his horse when he was killed. An outlaw popped out of the brush with a double-barreled shotgun aimed at Colbert's head. It hit his neck, blowing his head right off his body. The spooked horse then took off with the headless corpse still attached.

The former guerillas massacred every last one of the Choctaw men, but they were in for several surprises. The sacks of gold were empty. As it turned out, Colbert and his men had entered the wrong cave and came out empty-handed. In the darkness, it only appeared that the sacks were full of loot. The outlaws soon regretted their actions for another reason. In the nearby brush, they began to hear hoofbeats. Then, suddenly, only yards away, the horse with the headless rider dashed past them. The dead body should have fallen off the horse long ago. Not only that, to them, it looked as though the corpse was in command of the angry steed. The outlaws fled the area and never returned, though they made sure to tell the tale of their encounter to their friends.

Eventually, tales of the massacre reached the leaders of the Choctaw nation. Knowing the general area of the attack, they went to investigate, both to bury the dead and hopefully find the gold. They found three of the men, but no gold. Nor did they find Colbert's severed head. Or his horse. Or his headless body. Soon after, anyone who passed through the mountains was liable to see Colbert's angry, headless ghost race down the mountain on his horse. Until he was avenged, he was doomed to ride the mountain at night forever, the Choctaw believed. He was also destined to guard the treasure.

Over the years, several men braved the mountains to look for the lost gold. Among them was James Calhoun Meador, who hunted for the treasure under the endorsement of the Choctaw Nation, the agreement being that Meador could keep twenty percent if he found it. He never did, but he did see the headless horseman ride down the mountain on four different occasions.

After Meador gave up, next came James Barnett, who, unlike his predecessors, hit paydirt in

COWBOYS & ZOMBIES

October of 1893. While digging in a cave in the mountains, his shovel struck something hard. Barnett soon unearthed twenty $50 gold coins minted in the year 1858. This was indeed the lost treasure, which Barnett knew of being one-fourth Choctaw himself. The only problem was that Barnett was by then utterly exhausted. On the trail of the treasure, he had gone without food for three days and couldn't even think of excavating the whole cache. As such, he stored what gold coins that he could in the pockets of his overalls and stumbled down the mountain back to his camp. By sundown the next day, Barnett mustered enough strength to mount his horse and ride down the mountain. As he did, he heard ominous hoofbeats. He turned to see a headless rider storming by in the dusk, with just enough light present to make out the man's bloodstained shirt.

Barnett rode like mad for Tuskahoma and decided to leave the rest of the treasure where it laid. Two years later, Barnett had a change of heart. He was itching to get back to the gold. Maybe the headless rider had finally given up the ghost? Though it took three more years, Barnett eventually found his way back to the old cave in 1898. No sooner than he had re-found the entrance, there came the headless horseman dashing towards him again. That time Barnett left and didn't come back ever again.

Barnett was lucky compared to other men. Mysterious deaths seemed to plague the region, with men found dead as though they had been scared to death. Others committed suicide, it appeared. Was the headless rider to blame?

The tale only survived into the 20th century thanks to Maurice Kildare, who heard it from his grandfather, James Calhoun Meador. When Kildare asked his grandfather about the headless horseman for the last time, Meador simply replied, "Them mountains is filled with evil spirits."

FRONTIER TIMES ILLUSTRATION.

Sources:
Kildare, Maurice. "Kiamichi Warrior's Gold." *Frontier Times* (December-January 1972).

CHAPTER 9
THE WHISTLING ZOMBIE

ALTHOUGH TECHNICALLY A GHOST with supernatural powers, the South American specter known as El Silbón has a zombie-like appearance and a hankering for human flesh to go with it. The legend of El Silbón stemmed from Colombia and Venezuela, especially in the tropical grasslands collectively known as Los Llanos. Just as La Llorona is the crying woman, El Silbón is the whistling man, as his name literally means The Whistler.

El Silbón was usually depicted as a tall, lanky ghoul carrying a knapsack in which he kept human remains. Occasionally, the specter was gigantic, standing twenty feet tall amidst the trees. Other times, his creeping shadow was said to stretch out to grab his victims and he would eventually emerge from the shadow as he whistled. As stated before, he was quite zombie-like, with chunks of tattered flesh hanging from his emaciated frame. His signature attire comprised a straw hat and the bone-filled knapsack, said to creak as he walked. If a person was wandering alone at night and heard a whistling far, far away, they had better watch out, for that meant El Silbón was close at hand. However, if the whistling was close by, oddly enough, that meant the person was safe.

EL SILBÓN ILLUSTRATION c.1967.
https://factschology.com/mmm-podcast-articles/el-silbon-whistling-man

COWBOYS & ZOMBIES

El Silbón especially targeted unfaithful husbands and drunks. In the case of drunks, it was said that he would cut a hole in the drunk man's stomach, suck out all the alcohol, and then remove the man's bones to place in his knapsack. Worse yet, afterward, the man's soul was unable to cross over to the other side. Like El Silbón, they were cursed to wander Los Llanos for eternity until they could find El Silbón and reclaim their remains from his knapsack.

El Silbón's origin story was that of a spoiled brat son whose parents catered to his every whim. The family, comprising of the mother, father, and grandfather, all lived together in Los Llanos in the 18th century. His fateful transition occurred one night when he demanded venison for dinner and sent his father out to hunt a deer. When his father failed to return home, the son became impatient. The mother suggested that he go out and look for him in the woods, so the boy donned a knapsack, and off he went, whistling as he walked. Eventually, the boy found his father sans the prized meat.

The enraged teen took out his hunting knife and stabbed his father in spite of his apologies for not bagging a deer. He then cut out his father's heart and liver, tossing his remains in the knapsack to take home. The boy took them to his mother to cook and serve for dinner, claiming that they were the deer meat and that his father would be back soon. However, the mother noticed the organs were unusually tough for those of a deer, so she went to investigate and found her husband's bones and mutilated remains in her son's knapsack.

ENGRAVING BY JOSE GUADALUPE POSADA (1852-1913).

She ran to tell the grandfather of his grandson's horrid crime, and the grandfather had the boy captured and tied to a post. The mother put a curse on her son and the grandfather proceeded to whip his back. Then, he cleaned the open wounds with the most painful remedies he could, including lemon juice, chili peppers, and alcohol. The grandfather untied his grandson and placed upon his back the knapsack containing the remains of his murdered father. The grandfather put his own curse on the grandson that he carry his father's remains for all eternity. Lastly, he set two hunting dogs loose to chase the boy, who ran away to become El Silbón...[47]

---

[47] As to be expected, there are many versions of the tale, and in one the hunting dogs tore the boy apart on the spot rather than chasing him into the jungle. In yet another, the dog was more of a supernatural hellhound bound to chase him for eternity.

CHAPTER 10
THE OZARK HOWLER

SIMILAR TO THE Snarly Yow is the Ozark Howler. The creature is a true whatisit in the sense that it's been likened to everything from a werewolf to a hellhound and even a type of monstrous feline. It is more so defined by its howl, hence the name, than its appearance. The unique howl has been described as a cross between an elk's bugle and a wolf's howl. The body is about the size of a bear's, and naturally quite hairy. It is a quadruped with stocky legs and typically has a pair of horns atop its head. Almost always, it is black or brown in color, and in some accounts, its eyes glow ominously. It arose to prominence in the 1950s like many other cryptid monsters, but the earliest known folktale of the beast dates back to the early 1800s.

ENGRAVED PORTRAIT OF DANIEL BOONE.

Likely a purely folkloric tall tale, it asserted that none other than Daniel Boone took a shot at the monster in Missouri. The pedigree of the tale isn't complete hearsay, though. Boone enjoyed telling tall tales, which were usually just that. One of Boone's biographers, John Mack Faragher, probably pinpointed the origin of the "Boone vs. the Ozark Howler" story in *Daniel Boone: The Life and Legend of an American Pioneer.*

Supposedly, Boone was visiting his cousin, Jacob Boone, in Limestone, Kentucky, when he told a young boy of the time he fought a hairy creature called the Yahoo. Described as a ten-foot hairy giant, it seemed more akin to a Sasquatch than the Ozark Howler. And besides, the Yahoos were taken from one of Boone's favorite books: *Gulliver's Travels*. The tale of Boone fighting a hairy whatsit in the woods was "repeated to a number of people during his last year, one such as he would have told in a winter camp."[48]

POSTCARD OF THE OZARK MOUNTAINS OF MISSOURI.

Encounters with Daniel Boone or not, a hairy monster certainly stalks the Ozark Mountains. If anything, the Ozark Howler probably has more in common with devil dogs than it does anything else. In fact, it's been postulated that the Ozark Howler of late is actually the Irish hellhound of old.

---

[48] Faragher, *Daniel Boone*, p.309.

As European settlers—more specifically Scottish, Irish, and English—arrived in the Ozarks in the mid-nineteenth century, it's thought that tales of their hellhounds were transplanted along with them. Like hellhounds the world over, they had their own distinct variety, that being the Cù Sìth of Scotland. Though it had the overall appearance of a wolf, it was as big as a bull with especially shaggy hair. Its color was either a hellish dark green, like Greek-fire, or sometimes it was white, like the Cadejo, a hellhound from Mexico. Though wolf-like, the tail was long enough to coil, and would sometimes be reported as braided. (Some likened the tail to that of a lion's it was so long.) Its huge paws were as big as a man's hand.

Like the Ozark Howler, it had a unique sound associated with it. The Cù Sìth would let out three bays in a row that were so loud they could be heard for miles away. Some even claimed that they could hear it all the way out at sea. If you heard the bark of the creature, that meant you had better start running for safety, for upon the third bay, you would either be caught by the creature or die from fright alone. In much the same way that a Cù Sìth could take one to hell, others thought it might abduct you and take you to Magonia, the fairy realm.

A very direct link between the Ozark Howler and hellhounds came when the Cumberland Presbyterian Church in Russellville, Arkansas, decided to depict the Ozark Howler in a stained glass window. However, according to lore, a newly arrived pastor felt the image was demonic and ordered that it be taken down. It was, and shortly after, the church burned down. (Hellhounds, like Black Shuck, had a propensity for menacing local churches, hence the connection.)

Some indicate that the Ozark Howler is more tangent to the werewolf or skinwalker in that it is actually a shapeshifting witch or warlock. However, respected cryptozoologist Chad Arment asserts that the Ozark Howler is most likely just folklore. He's probably right.

Sources:

"Ozark Howler." Unlock the Ozarks.
https://www.unlocktheozarks.org/stories/folklore-legends-and-myths/ozark-howler/

Faragher, John Mack. *Daniel Boone: The Life and Legend of an American Pioneer.* Holt Paperbacks, 1993.

NEWSPAPER ILLUSTRATION OF CHIPITA'S GHOST.

CHAPTER 11
WALKING DEAD
OF THE NUECES

A TEXAS LEGEND tangent to La Llorona is that of Chipita Rodríguez. For many years, Chipita was notorious as the first woman to be legally hanged in Texas, and on Friday the 13th no less. She ran a small boarding house along the Nueces River in 1863 and was executed for brutally murdering a man—a crime she was likely innocent of. As it was, Chipita was an elderly woman who barely weighed 100 pounds when she was accused of the act.

Most sources say that Chipita was born in Mexico around New Year's Eve of 1799 and came to Texas with her father, who was part of the Mexican army during Santa Anna's march to San Antonio in 1836. However, her father, Pedro Rodríguez, deserted the army to take his wife and child to the

UNDATED NEWSPAPER PHOTO OF THE AREA WHERE CHIPITA WAS HANGED.

Nueces River near an Irish settlement called San Patricio. As Chipita grew to womanhood, legend holds that, like La Llorona, she married and had a baby. But unfortunately, her husband left her and took the baby with him. Now a spinster, Chipita ran a small boarding house, really more of a *jacal* (hut) along the Nueces River. During the Civil War in August of 1863, a horse trader named John Savage was passing through San Patricio on his way to Corpus Christi. At a local saloon, he bragged of a big sale he had recently made to the Confederate Army before going on to Chipita's jacal, where he stayed the night.

A few days later, Savage's corpse was found in a burlap bag floating down the river. His head had been split open by an ax. Bags containing $600 worth of gold coins belonging to Savage were found nearby, and the blame was placed on Chipita. She was arrested by Sheriff William B. Means and she repeatedly cried out, "No soy culpable." ("I am not guilty.") Also arrested was Chipita's slow-witted servant boy, Juan Silvera. Rumors circulated that not only was Silvera her illegitimate son, but that perhaps he had killed Savage.

ARTIST'S RENDITION OF CHIPITA.

As to why Chipita and Silvera were suspected, it was said that an ax was found covered in blood at Chipita's jacal. That she and Silvera often used that same ax to behead chickens wasn't a strong enough argument to get Chipita acquitted. Actually, Chipita didn't even receive representation at her trial, and nor could she speak English to the predominantly Irish townsfolk. The jury at Chipita's trial pleaded mercy for the old woman due to her age, but the judge would not have it.[49] While Silvera was sentenced to serve five years in prison, Chipita would be executed on November 13, 1863. On that day, she

---

[49] The judge was Benjamin F. Neal, later the first mayor of Corpus Christi.

was taken to a grove of trees along the river and hanged from the tallest oak they could find.

Ominously, one recounting stated that "a heavy, billowing gray mass rolled in from the Gulf and blotted out the sun."[50] Some even said that the poor old woman's legs were shackled as she marched to her doom.[51] Nor was it a swift death. She was placed on the back of an old ox cart, and when it pulled out from beneath her, it didn't snap her neck. Instead, she swung back and forth as she slowly strangled to death. Some accounts went that the hangman, John Gilpin, wrapped a bandana around her face, while others said no face coverings were used and onlookers watched in horror as Chipita's face contorted as she strangled. (Afterward, the villagers were so disgusted that they refused to help the hangman dig the grave.) Chipita was placed in a cypress coffin and buried under the hanging tree.

One man claimed he heard a ghostly wail come from the coffin before it was buried. Another rendition had the witness hearing a thump and a groan as though she was being buried alive. Odder yet, the tree was struck by lightning soon after the hanging, so that it withered and died. Some say nothing will grow near the spot where she was hanged, either. One of the Irish onlookers supposedly stated the following as they left the execution: "Tis a black day for San Patricio. Tis a

---

[50] McDaniel, "The Day They Hanged Chipita," *Kerrville Mountain Sun* (December 12, 1962), p.5.

[51] Because she had no dress for her hanging, one villager gave her an old wedding dress to wear, technically making her a Woman in White.

curse we have brought upon our town."[52] Perhaps they were right, for eventually San Patricio became a ghost town and today its claim to fame is Chipita, regarded as a wrongly accused fatality of frontier justice.

Like La Llorona, Chipita wandered and wailed along the local rivers for many years, sometimes seen with the noose still around her neck. "Many persons have claimed they saw Chipita walking slowly along the riverbank, the frayed noose dangling from her neck," said *The Baytown Sun* of June 13, 1960. In addition to the river, supposedly Chipita's ghost haunted Silvera, her servant boy, after he was released from prison. She was also seen in the boarding house of Miss Lida Dougherty in the 1930s. Miss Dougherty was said to remark of the execution, "Could a more unholy or unnatural thing have happened in an Irish village?"

Still, most saw her spectral shadow gliding near the site of her old jacal, forever calling out, "No soy culpable." Chipita's cries were heard, albeit much too late. She was officially pardoned in 1985, and a historical marker was placed near the site of her hanging in 2010.[53] Interestingly, since her pardon, sightings waned until the walking dead was seen no more.

---

[52] McDaniel, "The Day They Hanged Chipita," *Kerrville Mountain Sun* (December 12, 1962), p.5.

[53] About 25 years after her hanging, a 71-year-old man who was near death confessed that he had killed Savage all those years ago.

PORTRAIT OF ELIZABETH BÁTHORY.

CHAPTER 12
COUNTESS DRACULA OF LAS VEGAS

IN 1971, HAMMER STUDIOS released *Countess Dracula*. In it, Ingrid Pitt played the real-life figure of Countess Elizabeth Bathory, called Countess Dracula because in the film she used virgin blood to restore her youth. The movie was based upon the fantastical legend of Bathory, that being that she supposedly really did bathe in the blood of virgin maidens to stay young.

While the real Bathory never retained eternal youth, she was a noblewoman who was accused and convicted of the deaths of hundreds of women and girls between 1590 to 1610 in what is today Slovakia.

Interestingly, Las Vegas, New Mexico, has a similar tale of a Spanish noblewoman who attained eternal youth. Like the vampire tales recounted earlier in this tome, it too came from *Hispanic Legends from New Mexico*.

LAS VEGAS, NEW MEXICO, AS DEPICTED IN AN 1880 ENGRAVING.

The folktale was as follows:

Dona M. came from Spain. She was a very beautiful woman and she seemed to stay that way regardless of her age. After she had been here a number of years, her husband died and shortly thereafter she remarried. The man she married was about 15 years younger than she. People wondered.

After 15 years of marriage the people noticed how he had aged and she still remained young. She suddenly became very sick and the priest was called in. After hearing her confession, the priest came out of her room with a little box which he gave to her children with instructions to bury it where it could never be discovered again. It seems that this woman had made a pact with the devil and he had given her a box with magic lotions which enabled her to remain young.

In order for the woman to be cured, the priest made some holy water with which she was to bathe the woman. As the priest began to bathe the woman, she began to grow older and older and within the hour she was an old woman. She died the following day and friends and relatives who came to view the remains found it hard to recognize the woman.

This is a Las Vegas story told to me by one of my aunts and it was told to her by her father. The story is supposed to be true and many still hope to find the magic box.[54]

It's worth noting that the story ended similarly to *Countess Dracula*, which had Pitt's titular character reverting to her real age when she was denied the life-giving formula.

Sources:
Robe, Stanley L. *Hispanic Legends from New Mexico (Folklore and Mythology Studies: 31)*. University of California Press, 1980.

---

[54] Robe, *Hispanic Legends from New Mexico*, p. 211.

JOHN LEMAY

COMTE DE ST. GERMAIN.

CHAPTER 13
DISCIPLE OF COMTE SAINT GERMAIN

EVER SEE ONE OF THOSE vampire movies where either Bela Lugosi or Christopher Lee was unavailable to reprise Dracula, and so they simply did a spinoff? I'm speaking, of course, of films like *Son of Dracula,* which replaced Lugosi with Lon Chaney Jr., and *Brides of Dracula* from Hammer, which eschewed Lee's Dracula in favor of Peter Cushing's Van Helsing as the lead. In *Cowboys & Monsters,* I think that the most famous real "vampire" that I included was Jacques St. Germain, thought to really be Comte de St. Germain (b. 1691 – d. 1784). As such, I thought that, in the absence of more vampiric exploits from Germain, readers might enjoy this look into the life of one his disciples. But, before we get to the disciple of St. Germain, here is a little recap on Germain himself.

For some, Comte de St. Germain is a hero, while to others, he's more of a villain due to an alleged vampiric incident in 1904 New Orleans. In that case, "Jacques" St. Germain was living in New Orleans as a wealthy socialite... a wealthy socialite that often threw wild parties loaded with food that he, the host, never touched. Instead, he would only be glimpsed drinking from an ornate goblet. What exactly was in the goblet? Well, as Bela Lugosi once said as the title character in *Dracula*, "I never drink... wine." Adding to Germain's allure, he spoke of people who died hundreds of years ago as though he had actually known them. Then, there was the painting of his "ancestor," Comte de St. Germain, hanging on the wall that looked exactly like him. Naturally, people were fascinated by Jacques St. Germain and his mysterious past.

The high times at St. Germain's place came to an abrupt end one night when a prostitute flung herself from his balcony. As shocked onlookers ran to her aide, she told them how Germain had bitten her on the neck in a bid to drink her blood. She, being a lowly prostitute, was written off by the police, who didn't haul Germain in for questioning. They only asked that he come to the police station the following morning to make a statement, while the girl was carted off to the hospital. The next day, Germain never came. The police went to his house to find it devoid of his presence. After a thorough search, they turned up three very odd things. First, the wealthy man possessed not a single piece of silverware—it was always brought in by the caterers for his lavish parties. Next, they found bloodstained tablecloths. Lastly, and most revolting of all, they found wine bottles comprised of a mixture of wine and human blood.

"Jacques" St. Germain was never seen again, though Comte St. Germain was reported as being seen in Rome by Freemason C.W. Leadbeater. However, Rome was not St. Germain's current home, he was only visiting. And where was he currently living, you ask? Transylvania. There he lived in an old castle, performing magic rituals in a golden suit of armor draped with a purple cloak. St. Germain was next sighted atop Mt. Shasta, in California. Mt. Shasta is probably familiar to more than a few of you as the site of much supernatural activity.

It was on Mount Shasta that Germain communed with the focus of this chapter: Guy M. Ballard. In his day, Ballard was once described as a "Chicago fortune teller," but that's putting it mildly. Really, he was more of a cult leader who claimed to base most of his teachings on Germain. It's possible, of course, that Ballard never communed with St. Germain and just made the whole thing up. He was known to spend hours and hours in an occult library within Los Angeles, perhaps cherry-picking ideas he liked to create what would become known as the "I Am" movement.

As the *Dubuque Telegraph Herald* put it in their January 7, 1941 issue:

Guy M. Ballard, who was not what you'd call a religious man, founded [the I Am movement].

One day in 1929 he had a visitation by a spook called Saint Germain (no true saint, according to church records). Ballard, who at the time happened to be under indictment for some stock-selling activities in Illinois, was told by the vision that he was the incarnation of St. Germain and a fellow of such great purity and benevolence that he should spread the I AM gospel.

The newspaper left out an interesting aspect of the meeting, though; one that could tie into Germain's vampiric traits. According to the *Sydney Smiths Weekly* of June 05, 1948, Germain appeared to Ballard as "a young man and gave him to drink a cupful of 'creamy liquid' that appeared from nowhere. This liquid, the reader is informed, was 'delicious in taste and had an electrifying effect on the mind and body.'" If one didn't know better, they might be inclined to think this "electrifying" drink was blood-laced wine. In his own words in *Unveiled Mysteries*, Ballard said, "The moment I drank it—a sensation like lightning went through my body—carrying the feeling of its sparkling activity—into every vein."

Then, via astral projection, Ballard left his body to fly through the skies with Germain. (As he did so, a panther stood guard over his body while his spirit roamed the clouds.) Together, they flew to another mountain containing a secret underground city that pre-dated the sinking of Atlantis according to Germain.

After this, Ballard went on to found what was essentially the first of the "ascended master" teachings which led people to believe that they were reincarnated, ascended beings. Ballard, for instance, claimed he was a reincarnated George Washington among other figures. Ballard called his iteration of the philosophy the I AM movement. In nearly a decade's time, he and his movement had amassed nearly one

'I Am' Leader Sued

(Story starts on page 1.)

Guy W. Ballard, high priest of the I Am cult, and his wife, Edna, his high priestess. Ballard was sued again yesterday by a former disciple who charged conspiracy and intent to defraud.

million followers![55] Along with his wife, Edna, Ballard made a killing off of his followers.

Among their more wild claims was that a massive "gas belts" existed under the United States which could cause massive earthquakes. These earthquakes were forestalled by the I AM movement by transmuting these "gas belts" into "pure metallic gold"... somehow.

---

[55] Today it is still active under the name of the Saint Germain Foundation.

Great I Am Says He Owes No One

[TRIBUNE Photo.]
Guy Ballard, leader of the Great I Am cult, before his flock in the Civic Opera house yesterday, denouncing woman who sued him and assailing enemies of his movement.

Speaking of gold, St. Germain revealed to Ballard the site of several lost gold mines in Colorado. Once, Ballard was given a vision of a room filled with gold coins and nuggets. Towards the end of his life, Ballard began a scam revolving around a "lake of gold" that he had found somewhere. By 1938, Ballard was being sued for

$10,906.55 by a woman who had lost $6,775 to his probably non-existent Lake of Gold. The *Chicago Tribune* of September 30, 1939, explained that the woman was "induced by their 'mutual interest in mysticism and the occult arts and sciences' to help him buy the lake. She gave him the money, she thought, to buy up the last 7,000 acres needed to pump out the gold and other minerals."

GUY AND EDNA BALLARD.

It wasn't long before the Ballards and their fellow cultists began putting curses on people and organizations. According to his 1940 obituary, in October of 1938, Ballard "against all skeptics, put a curse of ghost steers, ghost pigs and ghost sheep on Chicago..." (This is what in particular caught my interest in Ballard and his cult, a curse of ghost steers.[56])

Ballard considered anyone in the Chicago area who "opposed his light" to be an enemy, and he and his followers would often "blast" them by chanting curses. Ballard threatened to send "the cows and pigs and lambs who have been deprived of life in [their] stockyards to haunt them." After this, his followers would shout: "Annihilate! Annihilate! Annihilate!" They also claimed that a lethal death ray would strike reporters who wrote ill of them.

According to articles, Ballard himself proclaimed to be St. Germain and also that he was immortal. Since Ballard's death from arteriosclerosis on December 29, 1939, would prove this false, Edna had him cremated as quickly as possible and told his followers that he had ascended on New Year's Eve. A bit later, Edna would find herself in the middle of a lawsuit for copyright infringement by the family/estate of Frederick Spencer Oliver (1866-1899), author of the novel *A Dweller on*

---

[56] Ghost steers were uniquely Southwestern for the most part, such as the Texas tale of Ghost Riders in the Sky, where a horde of spectral steers would incite stampedes leading to the death of humans and livestock alike.

COWBOYS & ZOMBIES

Two Planets. Though they were able to get out of that one, in 1942 they were on trial for eighteen counts of mail fraud. The matter wasn't settled until a full four years later when the Supreme Court vacated the fraud conviction on the basis that women were excluded from the jury panel in her trial. In 1942, Edna also moved to Santa Fe, New Mexico, the western branch of the Saint Germain Press.

Unlike his master, no one claims ghostly sightings or communions with Ballard, that I know of at least.

DOG WITH A HUMAN FACE.

Strange Monstrosity Seen by Many Persons in Colorado Hills—Attempt Capture in Vain.

Buena Vista, Col.—A strange animal roaming the hills in the vicinity of Wildhorse, a station on the Colorado Midland railway, two miles west of this city, has been seen a number of times by various people and has been described differently by each one.

The most startling of all, however, was the experience of a prominent ranchwoman last evening. She was driving slowly along the road across the Arkansas river, from where the animal has its lair, when her horse suddenly shied, almost throwing her from the rig. She was horrified to see, a few feet ahead of her and in the middle of the road, the monstrosity.

CHAPTER 14
WEREWOLVES & HELLHOUNDS OF THE GREATER SOUTHWEST

SINCE THE SKINWALKERS of the Southwest have been covered quite well, this chapter will outline a few tales of what would seem to be more traditional werewolves across the western states from Colorado to California, starting with the former. This article, printed in the *Sedalia Evening Democrat* (in addition to many other papers) on May 4, 1905, would seem to chronicle a werewolf:

A STRANGE ANIMAL
It Has Almost Human Face and a Red Mustache.

A strange animal roaming the hills in the vicinity of Wildhorse, a station on the Colorado Midland railway, two miles west of this city, has been seen a number of times by various people and has been described differently by each one, writes the Buena Vista, Col., correspondent of the Denver Times.

The most startling of all, however, was the experience of a prominent ranchwoman last evening. She was driving slowly along the road across the Arkansas river, from where the animal has its lair, when her horse suddenly shied, almost throwing her from the rig. She was horrified to see, a few feet ahead of her and in the middle of the road, the monstrosity.

It was about the size and build of a full-grown greyhound and of a drab color, its glistening sides covered with black spots as large as silver dollars. It had a long, smooth tail and the lady declares it had an almost human face and was evidently of a male gender, as a bristling red mustache ornamented the proper place upon its physiognomy. The eyes were close together and deep set and its ears stood erect and were very pointed. After a moment it uttered a piteous cry and slunk away through the brush, turning at the top of the hill for a last look. It stood erect on its hind feet, punctured the rarefied atmosphere with sounds that reverberated among the crags and compelled a pace on the part of the usually staid horse that was a revelation to the driver. A number of hunting parties have tried in vain to kill this animal and efforts are now being made to capture it alive.

COWBOYS & ZOMBIES

While southern Colorado has a great deal in common with northern New Mexico in regard to folkloric belief, it should be noted that the little community of Wildhorse was located on the far eastern edge of central Colorado near the border with Kansas. As such, it had no traces of Hispanic folklore, and the red mustache was a rather interesting flourish, to say the least. If anything, it bore some resemblance to the Kentucky Dog Eater than ran wild in the late 1800s. And, before moving on, I found no other mention of Colorado-based "strange animal" sightings in 1905, despite the article's mentioning of other sightings.

THAT MOST WONDERFUL ANIMAL.

THE "DOG EATER" IN *THE EVENING TIMES* OF OCTOBER 28, 1893.

New Mexico had no shortage of what could have been either werewolves or hellhounds, aided along by its mix of early-day Spanish and Native American beliefs. *Hispanic Legends from New Mexico* included several notable accounts of encounters with dogmen, like this one:

This incident happened in Rainsville, New Mexico. One night a young man who had gotten into the habit of drinking very much was going home. He had to pass through a deep ravine on his way home. When he got to the bottom of the ravine he saw the figure of a dog with red eyes, standing on his hind legs, approach him and he had a fight with the figure.

When he arrived at home after getting away from the figure, his clothes were all torn and he was bleeding from teeth marks. His parents and some friends went to look for the figure and when they reached the spot of the fight, they found only horse tracks.[57]

From the same tome came this tale, with a young man from northern New Mexico on his way to Pueblo, Colorado:

People engaged a young man as a watchman. One day a young man said he was going to Pueblo. He spent the night with his sweetheart. At dawn he started back, saw a black dog, and it chased him. He shot and killed the dog. When

---

[57] Robe, *Hispanic Legends from New Mexico*, pp.85-86.

he skinned the dog, he found a person inside. That is why they say people of Santo Domingo and Tasuki turn into dogs.[58]

PUEBLO, COLORADO.

On the same page was printed this account, as well:

It was late one evening when J. decided to visit his neighbors who lived across the river. As he approached the river, a huge dog trotted from under the bridge towards him. His instinct told him that this was no ordinary animal and he immediately hastened his pace. Each time he glanced behind him, he realized the dog was following him closely. J. reached for his knife and braced himself for the inevitable tussle. The dog pounced upon him and both threshed about for endless moments. Suddenly the dog

[58] Ibid, p.347.

uttered an agonizing cry and limped away. J. was badly shaken but well in other respects. A few days later a small boy found a woman's body body by the river. Her death was attributed to stab wounds.[59]

H-1340 ON THE BELEN CUT-OFF BETWEEN CLOVIS AND VAUGHN, N. M.

POSTCARD FROM VAUGHN, NEW MEXICO.

This interesting tale was collected from Vaughn, known as the crossroads of New Mexico. (And we all know how crossroads can be...) It was also unique in that it featured a werecat rather than a werewolf. As was usual in New Mexico, the wereanimal, in this case, was definitely a witch.

A. was 20 years old, a very quiet and enviable girl. She complained of a headache one morning and was dead late that night. While they were having *el velorio* [the wake] the following night, a strange animal walked in. It

---

[59] Ibid.

looked like a woman and at the same time resembled a wildcat. It went up to the coffin and pulled A.'s body out. The men went to get her back and the animal changed into a complete wildcat. [The girl's] father reached for the rifle, shot the cat and killed it. The cat turned into an old, wrinkled woman just as its back touched the floor. She admitted being a witch and wanted forgiveness for all she had done.[60]

Moving on to California, an account of what appeared to be a vegetarian werewolf was published in *The Hermit of Siskiyou*, a short book by L.W. Musick from 1896. In a footnote, the book related the following:

Note 1. A Del Norte Record Correspondent writing from Happy Camp, Siskiyou County, Jan. 2, 1886, discourses as follows:
I do not remember to have seen any reference to the 'Wild Man' which haunts this part of the country, so I shall allude to him briefly. Not a great while since, Mr. Jack Dover, one of our most trustworthy citizens, while hunting saw an object standing one hundred and fifty yards from him picking berries and tender shoots from the bushes.
  The thing was of gigantic size; about seven feet high, with a bull dog head, short ears and long hair; it was also furnished with a beard, and was free from hair on such parts of his body as is

---

[60] Ibid, pp.364-365.

common among men. Its voice was shrill, or soprano, and very human, like that of a woman in great fear. Mr. Dover could not see its footprints as it walked on hard soil. He aimed his gun at the animal, or whatever it was, but because it was so human would not shoot. The range of the curiosity is between Marble Mountain and the vicinity of Happy Camp. A number of people have seen it and all agree in their descriptions except some make it taller than others. It is apparently herbivorous and makes winter quarters in some caves of Marble Mountain.

Sources:
Musick, L.W. *The Hermit of Siskiyou.* 1896.

Robe, Stanley L. *Hispanic Legends from New Mexico (Folklore and Mythology Studies: 31).* University of California Press, 1980.

CHAPTER 15
THE HEADLESS WARRIOR OF THE CHEYENNE

IT'S DEBATABLE WHETHER or not the undead warrior presented in this chapter was an actual supernatural being, or simply the result of a freak occurrence involving the last spasms of a dying man. Whether it was the former or the latter, those who survived to tell the tale believed it to have been supernatural. The undead warrior in question was named Mouse's Road, a Cheyenne who was said to come back to life after being decapitated in battle.

The story has two major sources, the better-known one being George Bird Grinnell's 1915 book *The Fighting Cheyennes*. The other is a *True West* article, "The Headless Warrior" by William R. Brock, that appeared in the May-June issue of 1959. In that case, Brock claimed to have heard the tale directly from Mouse's Road's great-grandson, though he acknowledged that the tale had been printed before in *The Fighting Cheyennes*. But, being in *True West*, naturally Brock's version was the more dramatic rendition of the event.

Brock began his piece by comparing it to "Washington Irving's spooky tale of The Headless Horseman," which he noted was likely "pure myth." Brock continued, "...but in the annals of Indian history there lies the story of the headless warrior – a man so brave that even though he was beheaded in battle, he arose again to fight; a man whose bravery struck terror in an entire Indian village, drove its braves from their camp and marked his name as one never to be forgotten."[61]

However, while the corpse of Mouse's Road was said to sit up, he did not get up to fight again per the more sensational version published by Brock. As such, the original version from Grinnell shall be reprinted below:

The Death of Mouse's Road

In 1837, the year before the great fight with the Kiowas and Comanches, the Cheyennes were camped on the South Platte River. A war party of fourteen started south on foot to take horses from the Kiowas and Comanches. Stone Forehead and Pushing Ahead were the two who carried the pipes — the leaders.

---

[61] Brock, "The Headless Warrior," *True West* (May-June 1959), p.17.

COWBOYS & ZOMBIES

They found the camp of the enemy at the head of what the Cheyennes called Big Sand Creek, which runs into the Red River (of Texas). That night the Cheyennes went into the camp in couples. Stone Forehead was with a man named Angry. It was very dark. Close behind a lodge which they passed stood a pole with a shield hanging to it. Angry untied the shield from the pole and put it on his back, and they went on looking for horses. They came to a bunch of fifty or sixty, and went around them and drove them a little way, and each caught a gentle horse, mounted it, and drove off the herd.

When they reached the place where it had been agreed that they should meet, they found the others of the party already there, excepting only six men. Stone Forehead said: "We cannot wait here; we must start." They did so. Stone Forehead and Pushing Ahead went behind, where it is the custom for the leaders to travel, while the others went ahead. They drove their bunches along side by side, but two or three hundred yards apart. When day came they looked carefully at their horses so that they should know them again, and then they bunched the horses into a single herd. The way was so rough that they drove very slowly, and Pushing Ahead, who knew the country, kept saying: "We are going so slowly that they will surely overtake us."

It was a little past the middle of the day when they saw the Kiowas and Comanches coming.

There were only a few of them — not over thirty. Then the Cheyennes began to catch the swiftest horses, so that they could get about quickly. Pushing Ahead was a brave man. He said: "We must not let them take our horses. I do not think there are many of them." The Cheyennes mounted the fast horses and bunched up the herd, and, sending two young men ahead to ride one on each side so as to hold the horses together, they stopped. One of the Cheyennes got off his horse and fired at a Comanche, and shot his horse through the body. The Comanche rode back, and soon his horse began to stagger, and the Comanche left it and mounted behind one of his fellows. Then the Cheyennes made a charge on the Kiowas and Comanches, and they turned about and went back.

Of the other six men two, Little Wolf and his partner, Walking Coyote, were alone. They were on the head of the Washita, in level country. They had taken only a few horses. They saw a big party of Kiowas and Comanches coming in two bands. There was a ravine near them, and Little Wolf said: "These horses are tired out. We cannot drive them much farther; the enemy will soon overtake us. Let us dismount and hide in this ravine." They ran down the ravine and hid in a little hollow, and lay there. If the Kiowas had looked for them they would have found them, but just then they saw the four other Cheyennes far off, and turned to rush to them. Little Wolf and

Walking Coyote stayed there till night, and then set off for home on foot.

When the Kiowas and Comanches charged Mouse's Road and his three companions, the Cheyennes did not run; they rode up on a little hill and got off their horses and began to kill them. They had already left behind the horses they had taken and had only those that they were riding. Now, as the Kiowas and Comanche came up, the Cheyennes were seen to be taking off their leggings so that they could run fast and easily. The enemy charged them, and the Cheyennes fought bravely, though they had but few arrows, for they had been out a long time. In a little while the enemy had killed three of the Cheyennes.

Early in the fight Mouse's Road's bow was broken in two by a ball, and he threw it away. A Comanche chief, seeing him thus disarmed, charged up to kill him with his lance, but Mouse's Road avoided the blow, caught hold of the Comanche, pulled him from his horse, and killed him with his knife. Mouse's Road was still unwounded. He let the Comanche's horse go, and signed to the Kiowas: "Come on."

There was a man named Lone Wolf, a chief, and a brave man, who had been behind the other Kiowas. He called out; "I have just come and I wish you all to look at me. I intend to kill that man." He said to a Mexican captive: "Do you ride close behind me." The two charged upon Mouse's Road, and the Mexican rode straight at him, but Mouse's Road, though on foot, did not run away; he ran to meet the Mexican and, springing at him, seized him, pulled him from his horse, and plunged his knife into him several times. While he was doing this Lone Wolf dismounted and rushed up to help the Mexican. Mouse's Road dropped the dead Mexican and rushed at Lone Wolf, who ran at him with his lance held in both hands above his head, so as to deal a blow of great force. As he thrust with the lance Mouse's Road stooped and ran under the lance, caught Lone Wolf by the left shoulder, and struck him a terrible blow with his knife in the hip. Lone Wolf turned to run and Mouse's Road caught him by his hair ornament and with all his force thrust at his back. The knife struck one of the silver hair plates and broke in two, leaving about four inches of the blade on the handle. Lone Wolf screamed for help to his people, but no one came, and Mouse's Road continued to stab and hack and cut him with the stump of the knife until Lone Wolf fell to the ground, pretending to be dead.

Now came a Comanche chief riding a fine horse, and armed with a lance and bow and arrows. Mouse's Road took up the lance Lone Wolf had dropped, and ran to meet the Comanche. He parried the Comanche's lance thrust and drove his own lance into the Comanche and lifted him high out of the saddle, and the Comanche died.

Now the Kiowas and Comanches saw something that they never had seen before — a man who seemed swifter than a horse, more active than a panther, as strong as a bear, and one against whom weapons seemed useless. There were more than a hundred of the Kiowas and Comanches, and only one Cheyenne on foot, without arms, but the Kiowas and Comanches began to run away. Others, braver, made signs to Mouse's Road, who had now mounted the Comanche's horse: "Hold on I wait, wait. Take that horse that you have. We will give you a saddle. Go on home to your village and tell your people what has happened."

"No," signed Mouse's Road, "I will not go home; my brothers have all been killed and if I were to go home I should be crying all the time — mourning for these men. You must kill me."

When he said this all the Kiowas started to run, and Mouse's Road charged them. Behind the main body of the enemy were two Kiowas who had just come up. Both had guns, and when they saw Mouse's Road coming they got off their horses and sat down and waited until he was close to them, and then both fired. One of the balls broke his thigh, and he fell from his horse. Yet still he sat up to defend himself with his lance, and the Kiowas and Comanches, though they surrounded him, dared not go near him. One crept up from behind and shot him in the back, and he fell over. Then all the Kiowas and Comanches rushed on him and cut of his head, and when they had done that Mouse's Road raised himself and sat upright.

The Kiowas and Comanches jumped on their horses in fright, and fled to their village and told the people they had killed a medicine man and he had come to life again, and was coming to attack them. And, the women swiftly packing up a few of their things, the whole camp moved away, leaving many of their lodges standing.

This is the story told by the Kiowas. The Cheyennes have no account of it, for all the Cheyennes were killed. Lone Wolf lived for a long time, scarred and crippled from the cutting he had received. He died not long ago. The Kiowas and Comanches said that Mouse's Road was the bravest man they ever saw or heard of.

THE ORIGINAL ARTWORK BY JOE GRANDES THAT APPEARED IN THE 1959 *TRUE WEST* ARTICLE.

Though Brock, in his article, enjoyed the more fantastical elements of the story, he did admit that the resurrection "was undoubtedly caused by a reflex reaction, similar to that of a chicken when decapitated [and] the superstitious Indians thought that Mouse's Road's spirit was rising up to fight once more!"[62]

---

[62] Ibid, p.36.

JOHN LEMAY

Sources:
Brock, William R. "The Headless Warrior." *True West* (May-June 1959).

Grinnell, George Bird. *The Fighting Cheyennes.* 1915.

CHAPTER 16
ZOMBIE STEER

IN THE FALL OF 1888, Colonel Jack Potter conducted a rather ominous trail drive. For years, a former lead steer of John Chisum's, named Old Ruidoso, had been the terror of the range. Wherever the steer trod, death and misfortune followed. As such, it was decreed to get Old Ruidoso out of the territory. And so, under a trail drive by Colonel Potter, Old Ruidoso was marched off for the slaughter, being loaded onto a train in the new railroad town of Amarillo, Texas. Potter was relieved to see Old Ruidoso board the train with the herd and to finally be shed of him. Upon returning to Fort Sumner, New Mexico, Potter and his men were told that the train had a freak accident, wrecking and killing men and cattle alike.

Long after the wreck of 1888, Old Ruidoso, whose corpse was not found among the dead cattle, was spotted across Texas and New Mexico. The thing was, Old Ruidoso was of such an age that he should have been dead by then. But he wasn't, and the revenant of the range proceeded to terrorize the western territories as he had in life.

**PECOS BOB OLINGER,
CREATOR OF THE ZOMBIE STEER.**

In real zombie lore, in many cases, rather than being reanimated corpses, zombies were human beings induced into a trance-like state while they were living. This was done via hexes and curses. It was the same with Old Ruidoso, who had been hexed in the 1870s by one of the chief villains of New Mexico Territory: Pecos Bob Olinger. So vile was Olinger, that reportedly his own mother stated that he was a murderer from the beginning and was glad when he finally bit the dust. Among Olinger's depredations were shooting several men in the back, and being the cruel jailer of Billy the Kid, who eventually killed Olinger. However, the worst thing Olinger ever did was to hex Old Ruidoso when he was just a normal, if not overly large, steer in John Chisum's herd.

DEPICTION OF OLD RUIDOSO FROM
THE CATTLEMAN MAGAZINE.

At some point in late 1877, Olinger was riding along the Pecos River when he spied Old Ruidoso near its banks. Olinger roped Old Ruidoso and then branded him with a skull and crossbones and put a hex on him: "Your appearance in the roundups from Horsehead Crossing to the Bosque Grande on the Pecos shall be a curse, and I wish you could live a hundred years. But when you are dead and gone, I hope that terrible below of yours will haunt the people. I know that this curse I am bestowing on you will contribute to the population of every boot-hill cemetery along the Pecos."[63]

SPOOKY DEAD TREE AT BOSQUE GRANDE, ONE OF OLD RUIDOSO'S HAUNTS.

Actually, even before Olinger's cursed skull and crossbones brand, Old Ruidoso had been branded with other strange brands, including a question mark, a snake, and a scorpion among the more notorious ones. Some tellers of this tall tale even like to say Olinger's hexed skull and crossbones brand was what helped to start the whole Lincoln County War, for it was shortly after Olinger branded Old Ruidoso that the war broke out on the range in February of 1878.

In any case, Old Ruidoso was seen as an omen of death by all who spotted him. For instance, in

---

[63] Potter, "Ruidoso," *The Cattleman* (1960).

one case, when the cursed steer was spotted at a cattle roundup on the West Mora Arroyo north of Roswell in 1886, one cowpoke said to another, "I expect hell will pop. I see the hoodoo steer over there."[64] And within twenty minutes two of the cowboys had gotten into an argument and one shot the other. Another tale, set just outside of Roswell at a place called Pilky Flats, says Old Ruidoso was spotted grazing with old man Pilky's milk cows. The next day the whole Pilky clan was found dead with doctors claiming it was due to poisoned alkali milk.

Old Ruidoso's grotesque, branded body was also what supposedly spooked a mule team being driven by the notorious gunfighter Clay Allison. "There's that damned hoodoo steer, I'm going to kill him!"[65] Allison was said to shout. But that's when the mules got spooked and the wagon wheel suddenly struck a salt bump and Allison was thrown from his wagon receiving a broken neck and dying soon thereafter, believing it to have been the curse of the devil steer.

After the train crash outside of Amarillo, Old Ruidoso returned to the ranges of New Mexico with a vengeance. Soon, settlers began telling tales of the bloodcurdling bellows of a steer they could hear up in the mountains, knowing they came from Old Ruidoso. A man named Vicente Otero, of Fort Sumner, was said to have been the first to see Old Ruidoso when he returned to New Mexico,

---

[64] Ibid.
[65] Ibid.

and as a result had been driven mad. Because of his encounter with the steer, it was said that he would get down on all fours and paw and bellow at the ground just like Old Ruidoso did.

WHITE SANDS BY DONNA BLAKE BIRCHELL.

More ominously, in 1896, Old Ruidoso was again spotted in the vicinity of White Sands. The next day, the lawyer Albert J. Fountain and his eight-year-old son, Henry, disappeared into the white sands never to be seen again. Were they victims of the zombie steer? In any case, while their abandoned wagon was found within a few weeks, to this day, their remains have yet to be found.

CHAPTER 17
GIANT BAT OF SIERRA BLANCA

AMONG THE MANY legends of New Mexico is one that claimed it was the original home and birthplace of the Aztec emperor, Montezuma. More of a magical medicine man in this iteration, stories of Montezuma in northern New Mexico were numerous. Most of them went that before leaving for Mexico, Montezuma left an immortality granting eternal flame in his wake. However, one of the most fantastic Montezuma stories of all came from Southeastern New Mexico and involved a monstrous vampire bat guarding the eternal flame.

The sole source of the story, so far as this author can tell, can only be attributed to the *St. Louis Globe Democrat*, which had a penchant for telling fantastic tales. The *Globe* story, entitled "Legend of the Sierra Blanca: The Mysterious Great White

Bat, Who Holds Full Sway There," made the rounds in 1901 and was retrieved in this instance from the *Evening Star* of February 9, 1901.

LEGEND OF THE SIERRA BLANCA.

The Mysterious Great White Bat, Who Holds Full Sway There.

From the St Louis Globe Democrat.

Half way up the Sierra Blanca peak, approaching it from the south, where the cedars and the spruce trees are thickest and the pinon grows in profusion, there is a perpendicular wall of rock. Go eastward to its end, turn around its jagged corner, and there is a narrow shelf rising rapidly several hundred feet and leading to a small, deep canyon, in which there is a very dense growth of trees. Dark is the shade and profuse the growth of ferns and mosses, and velvety under foot the dark soil made of the leaves that have fallen for ages. Go up this small canyon a few hundred yards; then stop and go no farther. Before you is the mouth of a canyon leading to the heart of the Sierra. Its height is equal to the height of three men, and its width is equal to four times its height, and so dense is the growth of trees at its mouth that little, if any, light can enter it. Within is blackness profound. At dusk there emerge from it clouds upon clouds of the winged bats, who return at the early dawn.

COWBOYS & ZOMBIES

The story began in northern New Mexico, in the vicinity of what is today the Rinconada Canyon Petroglyph National Monument, in the region near Albuquerque. As with most areas in New Mexico, its history, illustrated by petroglyphs on the rocks, is steeped in the Spanish conquest and the habitation of the Puebloans.

RINCONADA CANYON PETROGLYPH NATIONAL MONUMENT. (NPS PHOTO/DANIEL LEIFHEIT)

"About seven generations ago," began the 1901 article, a group of cross-wielding, robed Spanish priests accompanied by "strange warriors carrying thunder sticks" entered a village near the Rinconada, "where the inhabitants engraved their story on the rocks." The vague article even implied that Montezuma's eternal flame was located in an estufa near Rinconada rather than Pecos, which was traditionally its home. So the article went,

The strangers defiled there the sacred estufa, quenched the sacred fire and planted a crossed stick. They murdered all of the priests of the estufa but one, who lay sick in his house. In the middle of the night he who was sick crawled to the estufa, saved some of the live coals, and in his house fanned to life again the sacred fire. At the coming of dawn the [priests] seized the white-haired old priest. The soldiers tied him to the tail of a horse, dragged him through the village and beat him with a whip of bull's hide until he fell to the ground as one dead, and he lay there in the burning sunshine all day, unconscious and without food or water. As he lay thus, there came to him the spirit of Montezuma and whispered unto him: "Take thou the sacred fire to the abode of the great white bat, and there those that suffer for me shall see my face, their hurts be healed and their grievances avenged," and as the rays of the sun came over the Sierra Blanca and the gray mists of dawn were being transformed into banks of gold, ruby and silver, floating high above, there, in the innermost depth of the mountain, was burning the sacred fire.

Before going any further, it should be stated that southern New Mexico's Sierra Blanca most certainly cannot be seen all the way from northern New Mexico's Rinconada Canyon. But, this being a story told in the not-so-accountable golden age of newspapers, we shall proceed. The beaten priest of the sacred flame trekked, somehow, to Sierra

Blanca and entered the abode of the Great White Bat. Hanging within an "immense arched cavern" in the mountain, the paper described the gigantic bat as being "twice as large as the largest buffalo, and each of its wings has the length of ten varas..."

POSTCARD DEPICTING SIERRA BLANCA IN LINCOLN COUNTY, NEW MEXICO.

Two priests, accompanied by ten soldiers, trailed the old beaten priest by way of hounds to the mountain. They entered the sacred cavern, which was "100 varas high" and "lost in the blackness of night, they found the aged priest of Montezuma, praying before the sacred fire."

And they rushed forward with evil intent, when, with the roar of the hurricane, there came down from the dome of the cavern, like an arrow shot from a bow, the great white bat, and with one blow of his wings he struck all of them down. Seizing two steel-clad warriors in each claw and one in his mouth, he flew out of the cavern, and the flames of the sacred fire leaped high in salute as he passed. In a few moments he returned, seized five more and flew out, and again he returned, and seizing the two priests of the evil one, whose wails of agony could be heard reechoing through the cavern and its labyrinth of passages, he disappeared for a longer time. On his return he carried on his back the priests that had been slain in the sacred estufa of the Rinconado. He threw the dogs upon the sacred fire and went to sleep again in the dome of the cavern, awaiting the further summons of his master.

THOUGH NOT MENTIONED, IT'S POSSIBLE THAT THE CREATOR OF THIS TALE DREW INSPIRATION FOR THE GREAT WHITE BAT OF MONTEZUMA FROM THE BAT DEITY CAMAZOTZ FROM MAYAN MYTHOLOGY.

COWBOYS & ZOMBIES

Following that,

In the village, in the broad light of day, six graves opened, and six priests of Montezuma arose there from, mounted an invisible steed and disappeared in the skies. The strangers and the remaining priest who witnessed this crossed themselves and fled from the village. In the heart of the mountain there is yet burning the sacred fire and guarding it until the return of Montezuma are the seven priests of the Rinconada.

As further proof of the story, the *Globe Democrat* reported that a group of Comanche 100 miles to the south in the Guadalupe Mountains found "the bodies of ten strange warriors, whose armor was shattered into fragments and imbedded in the rotting flesh." The priests were nowhere to be found, and presumably had been devoured by the bat. The article then concluded by revealing the tale was told by a woman simply identified as Mariana, who had heard it from her great-grandfather.

Due to the fantastic nature of the story and its source via the *Globe Democrat*, it's my best guess that a writer with a loose grasp of New Mexico's geography and an understanding of Aztec mythology made the story up, as I have never heard any variation of it elsewhere.

DON'T LIKE THE TELEPHONE.

Indians Predict That "Little People" Inhabiting Mesa Verde Cliff Dwellings Will Destroy the Line.

The Indians living near the celebrated Mesa Verde in southwestern Colorado are interested in the outcome of their predictions about the telephone line which the Government has just completed into the Mesa Verde National Park. They declare that the poles won't stand, and that the wires won't talk. When asked why, they solemnly reply that the "little people" will permit no such uncanny things to come so near their ancient homes. Nor can they be persuaded to the contrary. The white men will see for themselves, pretty soon.

The Indians live in great awe of the prehistoric dwellings of the Mancos Valley, which are, by far, the finest and best preserved of any in the American southwest. They will not believe that it was Pueblo Indians, or any Indians, in fact, who, so long ago that the oldest traditions describe them as they now are, carved these wonderful cities out of the cliffs. They believe that spirits built the cliff dwellings, and that spirits still inhabit them. They reverently call these spirits the "little people."

For this reason it is difficult to induce Indians to approach the cliff dwellings. Whether or not the continued success of the Government telephone line will shake their superstitious faith remains to be seen.

THE SEMI-WEEKLY NEW ERA
OF AUGUST 14, 1915.

CHAPTER 18
LITTLE PEOPLE
OF MESA VERDE

BECAUSE THE MUMMIES of Montezuma Castle were covered earlier in this book, it seems appropriate to discuss a corroborating legend in the form of the Little People of Mesa Verde in Colorado. Although today it will be adamantly stated that the Anasazi built the cliff dwellings at Mesa Verde, in the early 1900s, it was commonly accepted folklore that the Little People had built the lost city in the desert.

And indeed, for many years it was a lost city until two cowboys discovered it by accident. It was during a snowstorm in the winter of 1888 that Charlie Mason and Richard Wetherill were riding their horses through the snow when they looked across a deep canyon to see what appeared to be a lost city in the distance.[66] Less than 20 years later, by 1906, Mesa Verde was a national park, which had been studied by multiple archaeologists and anthropologists.

As stated before, in the past, as opposed to the Anasazi, it was the Little People who built Mesa Verde. This is evidenced in the *Zanesville Signal* of December 1, 1949, when author Karl Scheufler wrote that "The Little People who built the city, and who lived here, were small enough so that a couple and a child might have occupied each

---

[66] It should be noted that prior to that, Padre Escalante, a Spanish priest seeking a shorter route from New Mexico to California in 1776, spotted the ruins by accident and it was he who named them Mesa Verde, meaning the green table.

room." (It's important to note that Scheufler mentioned the Little People with no preceding context as though the reader should be aware of their existence.)[67]

Likewise, in his 1950 article on Mesa Verde, Roy E. Dunne casually mentioned the Little People with no build-up either, again implying to this author that it was common folklore that the Little People were a part of Mesa Verde. In his article, Dunne mentioned how J. Walter Fewkes of the Bureau of American Ethnology had "established

---

[67] Earlier he had also specified that "The rooms are not spacious. The standard size, 6 x 9 rug of today would not fit in very many, if any of these rooms," implying that they were indeed inhabited by Little People.

much of the history of the 'Little People.'"[68] A bit later in the article, the author mentioned how "a dwarf mummy was found during exploration" in a place letter named Mummy House.

MESA VERDE BY ANSEL ADAMS.

Several articles in the early 1900s mentioned how Native Americans of the time tended to avoid Mesa

---

[68] *Delaware County Daily Times* (May 31, 1950) p.7.

Verde. While it wasn't unusual for many Native American tribes to have an aversion to the dead, in the case of Mesa Verde, it wasn't human remains they were wary of, but rather the Little People who still inhabited the dwellings either in spirit or corporeal form. One such article stated, "Indians of today shun the ruins of Mesa Verde. They believe them inhabited by spirits whom they called the Little People. It is vain to tell them that the Little People were their own ancestors; they refuse to believe it."[69]

The Dispatch's July 28, 1915 article entitled "Mesa Verde Prophets," predominantly about weather predictions by the Native Americans, mentioned that the Native Americans "never stay an hour longer than is necessary because of their dread of the 'Little People' whom they believe still inhabit, in spirit form, the prehistoric cliff dwellings that have made the Mancos Valley famous the world over."

The same day, the *Saybrook Gazette and Arrowsmith News* printed a far more interesting story, implying that the Little People were still active enough to interfere with the meddling of modern man in their territory. In a story simply entitled "DON'T LIKE THE TELEPHONE," it reported the following:

The Indians living near the celebrated Mesa Verde in southwestern Colorado are interested in the outcome of their predictions about the

---

[69] *Vernon County Censor* (July 26, 1916).

telephone line which the Government has just completed into the Mesa Verde National Park. They declare that the poles won't stand and that the wires won't talk. When asked why, they solemnly reply that the "Little People" will permit no such uncanny things to come so near their ancient homes. Nor can they be persuaded to the contrary. The white men will see for themselves, pretty soon.

The Indians live in great awe of the prehistoric dwellings of the Mancos Valley, which are, by far, the finest and best preserved of any in the American Southwest. They will not believe that it was Pueblo Indians, or any Indians in fact, who, so long ago that the oldest traditions describe them as they now are, carved these wonderful cities out of the cliffs. They believe that spirits built the cliff dwellings, and that spirits still inhabit them. They reverently call these spirits the "Little People."

For this reason it is difficult to induce Indians to approach the cliff dwellings. Whether or not the continued success of the government telephone line will shake their superstitious faith remains to be seen.

It's worth putting out there that writers of the time may not have understood that, possibly, the Native Americans didn't believe the Little People to be dead. Although it was harder to grasp for writers of the early 20th century, instead of being dead, the Little People possibly lived in another dimension unable to be seen by the human eye.

Author Stephanie Waters did her best to get to the bottom of the story in her book *Colorado Legends & Lore*. She wrote, "Supposedly, the Little People caused quite a commotion when the park first opened and even a decade later when telephone lines were being installed."[70] She said that when she called Mesa Verde to ask about the legends of the Little People that she was disconnected. She stated that she also never got a reply from the park either. "I have to admit it kind of made me wonder if the Little People were up to their legendary shenanigans. Or maybe the receptionist just assumed I was munching peyote buttons!"[71]

Sources:

Waters, Stephanie. *Colorado Legends & Lore: The Phantom Fiddler, Snow Snakes and Other Tales.* The History Press, 2014.

---

[70] Waters, *Colorado Legends & Lore*, p.35.

[71] Ibid, p.36. Furthermore, Waters also mentioned how in the book *Wind Song*, the author, Mary Summer Rain, claimed to have seen a live Little Person in recent years in Colorado's Woodland Park.

**APACHE MEDICINE MAN
IDENTIFIED AS "LOCO".**

CHAPTER 19
THE RESURRECTION OF
CHIEF DIABLO

IT'S DIFFICULT TO DECIDE where to start this story, but the most logical beginning is probably with the death of Chief Diablo, leader of the Cibecue Apache of Arizona. Chief Diablo was something of a controversial figure among his own people. On the one hand, they were angry at him in the past for working with the U.S. cavalry that kept them subdued. That came to an end when the government established the San Carlos reservation, which forced Diablo's Cibecue Apache to cohabitate with their enemies, the White Mountain Apache. In August of 1880, Diablo died in a battle with the White Mountain Apache.

GROUP OF COYOTERO NEAR FORT APACHE, c.1873.

More trouble came for the Cibecue Apache that same year when the soldiers decided to take a census of the reservation. It must be remembered that in many Native American cultures, the name was a powerful thing, not to be given out to strangers, and certainly not the whites. Likewise, the name of the dead was not to be spoken by anyone, not even family, lest the utterance of the name attract the dead spirit. This is why, when the idea for a census, wherein the names of the Apache would be recorded, some within the tribe were greatly incensed, namely a Coyotero medicine man known as Nock-ay-det-klinne, who incited a rebellion in the late summer of 1881.[72]

In the weeks leading up to the rebellion, Nock-ay-det-klinne claimed that to help the Coyotero in their struggle against the soldiers that he would raise the slain Chief Diablo from the dead.

---

[72] The Coyotero Apache were allied and related to the Cibicue Apache, it should be noted.

COWBOYS & ZOMBIES

"Knock-e-de-klinney, in his self-imposed righteous wrath, conceived the plan of raising from the dead, the warlike chieftain, Diablo, who rested near him and who would sweep the home of the Coyoteros of the hated whites..." wrote the *Arizona Republic* of April 18, 1928, many years after the fact.

While this may sound like folklore created by Anglos, testimony existed in the form of other reliable Apache that this resurrection of the dead was actually attempted. It was not, however, successful and when tensions exploded in the Battle of Cibecue Creek on August 30, 1881, the U.S. cavalry eventually emerged victorious. During the skirmish, several Apache scouts under the allegiance of Fort Apache mutinied to join their Coyotero brethren in battle. The historical ramifications of the fight had the White Mountain Apache leaving the reservation to join forces with Geronimo.

Events culminated in a fierce battle in September of 1881 wherein "six officers, and about one hundred men [were] slain," or so claimed the *Chicago Tribune*. Rumors spread like wildfire that all of Apacheria was about to rebel against the U.S. government, they might even join with the Navajo to do so. It seemed that the Southwest might be poised for a repeat of the Pueblo Revolt of the 1680s. However, it was mostly media hype to sell papers. Once the papers realized they could no longer get away with embellishing reports of the violence in Apacheria, editors swiftly returned to covering President Garfield's ailing health after his assassination.

Promised To Raise Dead

From the meager information that he was able to obtain, which, however, demanded further effort, it was learned that the medicine man, Knock - e - de - klinney, had promised the Indians who were under the former war chief Diablo, that he would be able to raise him from the dead and, as he was a valiant chief and would have power bestowed upon him by the Great Spirit with whom he had communed, he would lead them to victory and rid their land of all the hated whites.

In making this extraordinary promise, he admonished them to gather together at all times and repeat their war dances so that their war spirit might not flag and to be in readiness to answer the call of the great war chief Diablo. He promised that when the corn was ripe (September) he would go to the highest mountain and consult with the spirits and return with the leader they worshipped.

ARIZONA REPUBLIC OF APRIL 18, 1928.

With that historical context in mind, we can digress back to the particulars of the failed resurrection of Chief Diablo. If you read carefully in the passages ahead, you will see that it wasn't merely to be the spirit of the dead chief that Knock-e-de-klinne was to conjure, but Chief Diablo was to revive in the flesh somehow.

Per the *Arizona Republic* of April 18, 1928:

COWBOYS & ZOMBIES

Promised To Raise Dead

From the meager information that [the census taker for the army] was able to obtain, which, however, demanded further effort, it was learned that the medicine man, Knock-e-de-klinney, had promised the Indians who were under the former war chief Diablo, that he would be able to raise him from the dead and, as he was a valiant chief and would have power bestowed upon him by the Great Spirit with whom he had communed, he would lead them to victory and rid their land of all the hated whites.

In making this extraordinary promise, he admonished them to gather together at all times and repeat their war dances so that their war spirit might not flag and to be in readiness to answer the call of the great war chief Diablo. He promised that when the corn was ripe (September) he would go to the highest mountain and consult with the spirits and return with the leader they worshipped.

In regard to Diablo, it is well to state that about six months previously, he was killed by Al-chu-say, a war chief of Pedro's band, in a quarrel over gambling. It was known that for years there had been bad blood between the two, and at one of their meetings a quarrel began and Diablo was killed. Diablo was beloved by his clan and was known as a fearless foe and hated the whites bitterly. It was on the Cibicu that the medicine man lived who was bent upon making trouble and it was at this place the bucks of neighboring

EUGENE ASA CARR, ONE OF THE MILITARY COMMANDERS INVOLVED IN THE BATTLE OF CIBECUE.

bands gathered to engage in the nightly "ghost dance" and to listen with eagerness to the tales of the ranting exponent of mystic art for the destruction of all the whites through Diablo.

Whites Hold Peace

After camping close to the Indian camp, no effort was made to communicate with the sullen Indians, but the presence of strangers did not interfere with the vehement exhortations of the scheming old medicine doctor, for around the roaring fires in their camp he directed the weird and ghostly dance. A weird and ghostly dance, indeed.

The flickering lights danced in unison with the crouched forms of the excited demons. The crackling embers of the roaring blaze cried out and mingled with the voices of the singing braves. Ever and anon, the passing of the wrinkled hags between the fire light and the dancing demons gave vivid thoughts of witches and voodoo hags of yore. No one dared approach, yet the interpreter, our Loco Jim, gained the information that pointed to serious results in the near future.

Applauded by significant grunts, this really gifted Apache whose eloquent and fanatical utterances inflamed a tribe of peaceful Indians into a band of murderous savages, spoke as follows and directed to a visitor:

AN APACHE WARRIOR BY WILLIAM F. FARNY.

"Why should the paleface seek the haunts of the brave Coyotero with their bad medicine?

"The belief of the Coyotero is different.

"There was only one brave among us the Coyotero, who could keep the whites back—Diablo, the chieftain.

"His spirit hovers amid the rustling pine, the fluttering leaves denote his presence

"He Will Come Again."

"The wail of the lion and the roar of the bear tell you that he is near. He will come again, not in spirit, but in the flesh to deliver us from the hated whites.

"Diablo guards our interest. Diablo seeks a remedy for our sorrows. Diablo will live again. In the dance we seek inspiration. With gliding, swaying movement we commune with the spirits.

"The dance inspires passion, faith, fury, and strength. All this we will need at the resurrection of the great Diablo.

"Is it not I, who receives the message at the resting place of the bones of Diablo?"

After a series of chanting harangues far into the night, the tired dancers retired. This method of inciting a peaceful people had been going on for weeks and secrecy was one of the conditions imposed by the scheming medicine man.

From the scouts sufficient evidence of future trouble was gained and after a few hours the next day in the camp of Sanchez, counting what people we could in spite of the advice of Knock-e-de-klinney, we started for Salt River and on to San Carlos.

Knock-e-de-klinne claimed the recording of their names was "bad medicine," that to have their names on paper would make it easy for the devil to find them at any time; that they would not give the names of their women for the white men to locate and steal.

On arrival at San Carlos the true condition on the Cibicu was reported by the writer to the agent, J. C. Tiffany. That the matter was taken up in due form and presented to the authorities, it will be seen from correspondence to follow, that steps were taken to stop the influence of the agitator.

"They then ran off the animals, already turned out to graze.[73] The medicine man was killed as soon as they commenced firing, and we drove them off, after a severe fight, in which we lost Captain Hentig, who was shot in the back by our own Indians, as he turned to get his gun. Four privates were killed and one sergeant, and three privates wounded, two mortally. After burying the dead, I returned as quickly as possible, and arrived at the fort on the 31st, found that some of the Indians had preceded me and killed eight men on the road to Thomas. The day the soldiers retreated from the battlefield on the Cibicu, after burying their dead, the savage instinct of the Apache was aroused and, true to their custom, they in their revengeful ire, dug up the bodies of the fallen soldiers and crushed in the lifeless skulls with rocks and frightfully mutilated the bodies.[74] The whole tribe of the

[73] As an interesting aside, supposedly the one to run off the soldier's horses was none other than the deadly and beautiful Apache warrior woman, Lozen.

[74] Many Apache believed that one would roam the afterlife resembling how they last looked. Case in point, when

Coyoteros was on the war path, some active, yet all in sympathy and the whole country was aroused and on the defensive for many months until they surrendered in groups, the leaders of the mutinous scouts Deadshot, Dandy Jim and Skippy, being court-martialed and executed at Fort Grant.

As for the medicine man, the paper reported, "The body of Knock-e-de-klinney was gone—spirited away by the Apache ghouls..." That fantastic flourish aside, more accurate accounts stated that the medicine man was wounded in battle, and as he crawled across the ground, a soldier attacked and killed Knock-e-de-klinne with an ax.

However, there is one very interesting aside to the notion of Knock-e-de-klinne attempting to raise the dead. Per Ace Daklugie, son of Chief Juh, to historian Eve Ball, it may have actually happened. Daklugie claimed that during a Ghost Dance in the mountains, that Chief Nana told him that he saw Nock-ay-det-klinne conjure several dead chiefs up from the ground. As it was, Chief Juh and Chief Nana had both heard of Nock-ay-det-klinne's planned ghost dance and wanted to attend. In the words of Daklugie to Eve Ball:

Mangas Coloradas was beheaded by U.S. soldiers, the Apache were greatly angered because they believed that meant that Mangas was wandering the afterlife sans his head. As such, perhaps the Coyotero felt the dead soldiers would have to wander the afterlife in dismembered form.

Nana recounted that... After performing until almost morning, Noche-del-klinne had terminated the rite, and, accompanied by a few dancers, he started up an incline in the misty light. Before he reached the crest, he stopped and lifted his arms in prayer. Dimly those with him saw the bodies of three great chiefs – Mangas Coloradas, Cochise, and Victorio – rise slowly from the earth. When they had emerged and were visible to their knees, they slowly sank back. Nana said that he had seen this and the word of Nana was not to be questioned.[75]

ACE DAKLUGIE, RIGHT, WITH GERONIMO.

Likewise, another corroborating source existed in James Mooney's report, "The ghost dance religion and the Sioux outbreak of 1890," published in the 14th annual report of 1892 to 1893. Mooney stated that in June 1881, Nock-ay-det-

---

[75] Bal, *Indeh*, pp.53-54.

klinne planned to "bring back from the dead two chiefs who had been killed a few months before..." And Mooney also reported with certainty that the Ghost Dance "was kept up steadily at his camp on Cibicu Creek until August..."

**THE GHOST DANCE OF 1889–1891,
BY FREDERIC REMINGTON IN 1890.**

Furthermore, per the testimony of Ace Daklugie, Nock-ay-det-klinne was trying to prevent violence. He told Ball,

I believe that Cibicu is least understood by white people. Writers, using reports of military officers, believed that Noche-del-klinne was inciting the Indians to an uprising. He was attempting to do exactly the opposite; he was doing his best to prevent one. He did not invent the Ghost Dance... Apache Medicine Men had used it to remind us that Ussen had promised to rid the country of our enemies in His own way and at His own time. That seems to have been unintelligible to military officers and to historians.[76]

Overall, this serves as yet another fascinating example of how the truth gets misconstrued into fabulous folklore, in this case being that the medicine man wanted to resurrect Chief Diablo to wage war. It's also interesting to know, though, that Noche-del-klinne possibly did contact the long departed spirits of Victorio, Cochise, and Mangas Coloradas.

Sources:
Ball, Eve with Lynda Sanchez and Nora Henn. *Indeh: An Apache Odyssey.* University of Oklahoma Press, 1988.

---

[76] Ibid, p.52.

TERROR OF GREEN TOOTHED MONSTER

The Cucupira of Amazon Woods Is Bullet Proof, but Not Intelligent.

FOND OF HUMAN HEARTS

Brazilian Explorer Tells of the Peculiarities of Demon.

CHAPTER 20
GREEN-TOOTHED
VAMPIRE
OF THE AMAZON

SOUTH AMERICA HAS some interesting ties to zombie lore. For instance, the very word actually originated from an 1819 history of Brazil by poet Robert Southey as "zombi"—in fact just a reference to Afro-Brazilian rebel leader Zumbi. Folklorically speaking, Brazil's curupira has a few similarities with vampires and zombies.[77] Sometimes dwarfish in stature, the curupira were guardians of the Amazon rainforest who stalked poachers and hunters who took more than they needed. They also consumed human flesh.

The oldest mention of the curupira was by José de Anchieta, in São Vicente on May 30, 1560. He stated, "It's a well-known thing and it's rumored by

---

[77] The name *kuru'pir*, means "covered in blisters".

everyone that there are certain demons, which the Brazilians call corupira, that often attack Indians in the bush, whip them, hurt them and kill them."

He continued,

Our people are witnesses of this. Brothers, who sometimes saw those killed by them. Therefore, the Indians usually leave on a certain path, which leads through rough forests to the interior of the lands, on the top of the highest mountain, when they pass by, bird feathers, fans, arrows and other similar things as a kind of oblation, fervently begging the curupiras not to harm them.

CURUPIRA APPROACHING A SLEEPING WOMAN, MANOEL SANTIAGO c.1926

The Curupira received wide exposure in newspapers in the year 1908, when the following story was printed in various papers, though this specific rendition came from the *Great Bend Tribune* of June 27, 1908, and spelled it Cucupira:

COWBOYS & ZOMBIES

TERROR OF GREEN TOOTHED MONSTER.
THE CUCUPIRA OF AMAZON WOODS IS BULLET PROOF, BUT NOT INTELLIGENT.
IS FOND OF HUMAN HEARTS.

Brazilian Explorer of Wilds Tells of Peculiarities of Demon of Wilderness of Which Natives Are Deathly Afraid.

Washington. - "I had not been in Brazil for 24 hours before I heard of the Cucupira," says a man who has been in out-of-the-way parts of Brazil. "At Para you can enter the primeval forests in a three-minutes' walk from our hotel, and so it happens that one may lie in bed and hear the prowling denizens of the woods giving their nightly concert. I was told, even while there, that any particularly frightful cry was made by the cucupira.

"Just what the Cucupira was no one pretended to know. I was going up the river 600 miles to visit an old friend, and before going I read up about it.

Prof. C.F. Hartt of Cornell, in "The Mythology of Brazil," wrote: 'One of the most important among the myths of the Indians of Brazil is called in the Tupi language the Cucupira. In all parts of the country one hears of this evil spirit of the woods, but no good and exact description of it exists.'

"I'm Hungry, Give Me Your Heart to Eat."

ILLUSTRATION FROM *THE GREAT BEND TRIBUNE* OF JUNE 1908.

COWBOYS & ZOMBIES

"C.B.F. De Souza, in Valle de Amazonas, wrote in 1873: 'I believe it is certain that the Indians believe in the existence of a spirit or demon which appears in the woods and is called the Cucupira.'

"Mr. Bates, the naturalist, is quoted as saving: 'The Cucupira are both sexes and have children.'

"At the plantation of my friend, Capt. Manuel Valdez, I heard the same vague accounts of the creature. Almost every night at sunset, when the nightly concert begins, some one among his 30 employees would smilingly say, as he heard some particularly unearthly cry: 'That is a Cucupira.'

"To do justice to these people one must forget the impressions of tropical forests which he got from school geographies. Along the outskirts of the streams birds, butterflies and flowers are everywhere, and there is an incessant chatter and chirp of small birds. Go but a short distance and all is changed.

"One may walk for hours without seeing a living creature, and the silence is only broken by the harsh cries of macaws and parrots as they fly over or feed on the surface of the canopy of green, nearly 200 feet overhead. The forest is like a deserted cathedral and until sunset the silence is oppressive.

"But the moment the sun drops this silence is broken by sounds like the crash of a great orchestra. Even an educated man will feel that hidden all about him are creatures of which he can form no conception save by their frightful cries.

"In these solitudes, when the light is beginning to fall, and remembering the nightly pandemonium, it is not so hard to understand the origin and influence of the most absurd stories one has heard. For instance, a lost Indian hunter who had shot a large monkey lay down to rest and fell asleep. He was awakened by a strange creature, who proved to be a Cucupira.

"'What is the matter, brother?' the Cucupira asked, and sitting down beside him added: 'I am hungry, give me a piece of your heart to eat?'"

"Secretly reaching behind him, the hunter gave him the monkey's heart.

"That is good, now give your liver,' said the hungry demon.

"This was eaten also. Then the hunter said:

"I, too, am hungry: give me your heart and liver."

"The Cucupira, seeing that the man was uninjured, and not wishing to be outdone, took the hunter's knife and slashed out his two organs and fell down dead.

"Another hunter found a curious skeleton at the foot of a hollow tree. From the skull he removed one of the teeth, which were green, for a souvenir."

How much truth, if any, resided in the article is, as always, debatable.

CITY OF THE DEAD

This next tale, involving prehistoric mummies, took place in the Timber Lake region of South Dakota in April of 1922. It was published in the *Aberdeen Daily American* of April 15, 1922. Because I greatly doubt its authenticity I won't delve into an examination of it and will simply reprint it for your amusement:

Trapped by a blinding Dakota sleet storm without food or shelter, two Indian guides, John Stands On His Ear and his brother Joe, discovered one of the most mystic caves in America, brilliantly lighted from no apparent source of power, with walls carved with fascinating figures of Indian bells and fairies.

Like the poor little maiden in the dream books which every child has read, the Indian brothers were fighting a losing battle with the terrific storm. They turned loose their horses and sought shelter among the banks of the sluggish Missouri River; their clothes were wet and torn. Aimlessly they groped through the underbrush for a dry spot to rest their weary bones. They stepped into a hole; the hallway of fairyland but didn't know it.

John offered to lead the way. Down and down he crawled through the dark narrow passageway with Joe close at his heel. Suddenly they beheld an immense room, lighted like the mirrored stag of a Broadway cabaret. It was at least a mile long, half as wide and forty feet high. Near the entrance, as though thrown carelessly down by ancient warriors who had no use for them here, were large metal axes and spears with hilts of bone. On the south wall, near which was the opening from the outer world were startling drawings of great beasts, birds and reptiles such as had never been seen in pictures by the wandering men.

On this wall down toward the center of the great room was the life size painting of a woman seated in a 'throne' mounted on a strange looking beast. So marvelously had the artist wrought that the pictures seemed to stand out from the wall and for a moment the men were dominated by the feeling that they were standing in the living presence of a regal personage of another age.

The features of the woman were fair and strikingly beautiful. Her light brown hair hung loose, cape-like garment of mixed blue and gold. The beast resembled a horse; the head and the hoofs were cloven twice forming three blunt toes. Long the men gazed upon this masterpiece of an ancient mural artist and then turned to look upon the strangest and most startling thing yet disclosed. Near the center of the great room was a long stone table surrounded by about twenty chairs of like construction and in each chair, the upright mummified body of a human; the remains of a prehistoric people of giant stature.

COWBOYS & ZOMBIES

In the center of the table rested a huge bowl and on each side of it were two or three decanters. Each of the mummified bodies were smote with blood. Suddenly, from them came freezing moans and terrifying shrieks as though a million lost souls were voicing their lamentations. The men were no longer curious as to the furnishings of this age-old banquet hall. Their only desire on Earth was to again get on the outside of it and it is not unlikely that they straightened the hole some in making their exit from a place where they insist they would have had a view of the infernal regions had they the courage to remain. What they witnessed and heard were probably the products of the combined working of electricity and air currents but their views are so self-satisfying that it would be a shame to disabuse them were it not for the fact their assistance is needed if others are to have the privilege of visiting the most wonderful place.

When they emerged into the storm, they had but one thought in mind, and that was to travel the shortest route to the point farthest removed from where they were. They were picked up on the open prairie the next forenoon by another Indian, nearly dead from exposure, and taken to their home. All efforts to induce the men to assist in again locating the entrance to this cave of wonders having proving fruitless. They shake their heads and say that it is the earthly abode of the Evil Spirit and that misfortune might befall them if they again sought to find it.

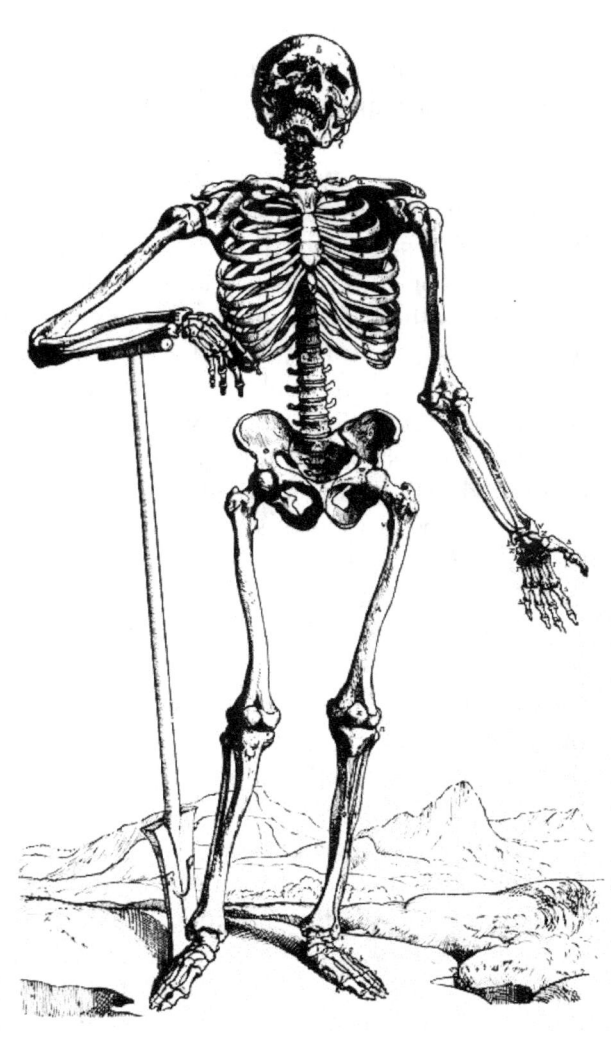

CHAPTER 21
BILLY THE KID
AND THE
MAD SCIENTIST

BILLY THE KID has some intriguing connections to Las Vegas, New Mexico. If some sources are to be believed, he met and gambled with Jesse James there in 1878. After his capture, in the early winter months of 1881, the Kid passed through Las Vegas via train, escorted by his jailer, Sheriff Pat Garrett. Odder yet, Billy may have returned to Las Vegas post-mortem thanks to what could be called a mad scientist. Said mad scientist was a "skelologist," someone who scraped dead bodies to get to the skeletons. As every western enthusiast knows, Billy the Kid was shot and killed by Pat Garrett around midnight on July 14, 1881, and buried the next morning. Per reports from the *Las Vegas Optic*, the Kid most certainly did not rest in peace, though.

PAINTING OF THE KID'S FUNERAL WHICH HANGS IN THE BILLY THE KID MUSEUM IN FORT SUMNER.

Months later, the September 10, 1881 edition of the *Las Vegas Optic* screamed: "The Kid Kidnapped—Or Rather His Mortal Remains Exhumed by Midnight Ghouls!"

The fifth day after the burial of the notorious young desperado [July 20th], a fearless skelologist of this county, whose name, for substantial reasons, cannot be divulged, proceeded to Sumner, and in the silent watches of the night, with the assistance of a compadre, dug up the remains of the once mighty youth and carried them off in their wagon. The "stiff" was brought in to Las Vegas, arriving here at two o'clock in the morning, and was slipped quietly into the private office of a practical "sawbones," who, by dint of diligent labor and careful watching to prevent detection, boiled and scraped the skin off the "plate" so as to secure the skull, which was seen by a reporter last evening. The body, or remains proper, was covered in dirt in the corral, where it will remain until decomposition shall have robbed the frame of its meat, when the body will be dug up again and the skeleton "fixed up"—hung together by wires and varnished with shellac to make it presentable. Then the physicians will feel that their labors have been rewarded, for the skeleton of a crack frontiersman does not grow on every bush, and the "bones" of such men as the Kid are hard to find. The skull is already "dressed," and is considered quite a relic in itself. The index finger of the right hand, it will be remembered, was presented to THE OPTIC at the time the exhumation was made. As this member has been sent east, the skeleton now in process of consummation will not be complete in its fingers; but the loss is so trivial that it will be hardly noticeable.[78]

Long before the September story, the *Las Vegas Daily Optic* of July 18th had reported that Dr. E.H. Skipwith of that city would "pay one hundred dollars for the 'Kid's' skeleton." As such, he emerged as the skelologist in question.

Billy's body may have been desirable not because he was a famous desperado, but simply because he

---

[78] The Kid's detached trigger finger was a reference to an earlier article, wherein it was put on display in a jar in the *Optic* office.

had no next of kin to object to the scientific study of his corpse. Back then, most states didn't have a legal process whereby one could donate their body to 'science' post-mortem. Therefore, medical students and doctors had great difficulty in procuring corpses for study. As such, they had to result to the Dr. Frankenstein method of grave robbing. (And, considering Billy was buried without any type of embalming in the hot New Mexico desert in the middle of summer, transporting his corpse by buckboard would have been a grotesque undertaking to say the least.)

THE KID'S FIRST MARKER WAS SIMPLY A CRUDE WOODEN CROSS, SEEN ABOVE.

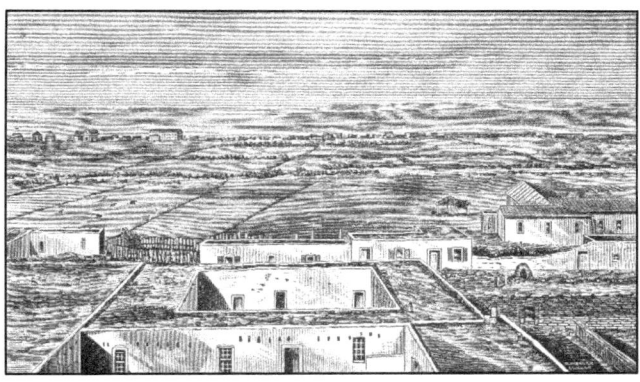

ILLUSTRATION OF WEST LAS VEGAS c.1880.

As to why Dr. Skipwith was never arrested for the act, most will simply say it's because it was a fake story to begin with. The late Dr. Robert Stahl investigated the story from every angle, though, and speculated that, if the story were true, then Skipwith may have threatened the editors of the *Optic* by way of canceling ads placed in the paper if they didn't drop the story. Though it can't be proven whether the skeleton was the Kid's, it was said that Skipwith had a complete human skeleton in his office above the First National Bank on the Plaza in Las Vegas until Skipwith moved to Roswell in 1889. Afterwards, it was likely given to Dr. William Tipton.

It is thought that Dr. Tipton, once referred to as the most "notorious body snatcher in New Mexico,"[79] aided Skipwith in his initial 1881 grave-

---

[79] In 1903, Dr. Tipton was outed in a scandal in the papers, alleging that an assortment of human bones had been found

robbing expedition into Fort Sumner. Tipton was born just a week shy of Halloween on October 23, 1854, in Missouri. Six years later, he had moved with his parents to Watrous, New Mexico, a little village steeped in the lore of witchcraft and were-animals. Perhaps the grim fairy tales of the region influenced an interest in the macabre, for eventually he became the medical superintendent of the New Mexico Insane Asylum in Las Vegas, built in 1892.

It is thought that just as the skeleton was passed on to him by Dr. Skipwith that Dr. Tipton, in turn, passed it along to a former student turned doctor, Miguel Frederick Des Marais. Dr. Stahl found corroborating evidence for this in the book *Las Vegas and Uncle Joe: The New Mexico I Remember.* In the book, Milton C. Nahm, a local boy, claimed to see a skeleton hanging around Des

---

scattered about the grounds of the New Mexico Insane Asylum. The June 27, 1903 *Daily Optic* reported:

The only case brought against the management of the asylum that could not absolutely be disproved was the charge that Dr. Tipton had carved the flesh from the body of Mary Leonard, a patient who died in the asylum, for the purpose of securing a skeleton. The bones were found scattered about the grounds outside the fence some time later. *The Advertiser* and the west side residents raised a terrible storm of indignation in this matter.

This prompted an investigation from Billy the Kid's old "pal," Governor Miguel Antonio Otero. Ultimately, Dr. Tipton was exonerated of all charges by the asylum board, headed by a member of the notorious Santa Fe Ring named Judge Elisha V. Long.

Marais's office in Las Vegas in the summer of either 1925 or 1926.

The skeleton was dangling from an old gas fixture in the middle of Des Marais's office. Upon seeing it, Nahm stated that "Somebody busted his wishbone for him and then patched it up . . . and the forefinger on the right hand is missing."[80] When Nahm asked Dr. Des Marais about the missing finger, he replied that it was actually the individual's "trigger finger.[81] This is doubly interesting considering that it was said that the trigger finger was removed from the Kid's hand post mortem and put on display in Las Vegas. Otherwise, Dr. Des Marais was elusive when pressed for further details, revealing neither where the skeleton came from or who it was in life. Tellingly, though, he told Nahm that if he looked up issues of the *Optic* from September of 1881—which, if you'll recall, reported on the theft of the Kid's corpse—then he would find the identity of the skeleton! If Des Marais was pulling his leg or not is unknown.

But what did Pat Garrett and the Kid's friends have to say about the supposed theft of his skeleton? According to Fort Sumner resident Charles Foor, the initial *Las Vegas Optic* newspaper articles caught the attention of Pat Garrett right away in 1881. A 1928 article in the *Southwestern Dispatch* related that "Mr. For [sic] said that he had inspected the grave in the company of Pat Garrett 18 months after the internment and

---

[80] Nahm, *Las Vegas and Uncle Joe*, p.97-105.
[81] Ibid.

when the first claim of the moving of the bones was made by the Las Vegas people. At that time both men agreed that the grave was untouched."

Billy the Kid's Grave, as it appears in 1929, and his two pals' graves on each side of him. Photo by A. M. Sparks, Winters, Texas.

One of Garrett's biographers, Richard O'Connor, claimed that Garret visited the grave several weeks later after his "indignation was aroused by reports that carnivals, dime museums, and other opportunistic enterprises were displaying what they claimed where parts of Billy's corpse." O'Connor also claimed that while there Garrett even dug up the body to make sure, but this is doubtful. Whatever the case, Garrett addressed the rumors in *Authentic Life*:

> I said that the body was buried in the cemetery at Ft. Sumner. I wish to add that it is there today intact—skull, fingers, toes, bones, and every hair on the head that was buried with the body on that 15th of July, doctors, newspaper editors, and paragraphers to the contrary now withstanding. Some presuming swindlers have claimed to have the Kid's skull on exhibition, or one of his fingers, or some other portion of his body, and one medical gentleman has persuaded credulous idiots that he has all the bones strung up on wires...Again I say the Kid's body lies undisturbed in the grave—and I speak of what I know.

"This is the Place," He Said — Where
Billy the Kid was Shot

**PAT GARRETT, ABOVE, RETURNING TO
FORT SUMNER IN THE EARLY 1900s.**

Whether Garrett was right, or the *Optic* was, is anyone's guess at this point.

Sources:

Garrett, Patrick F. *The Authentic Life of Billy the Kid.* New Mexico Printing and Publishing Company, 1882.

Nahm, Milton C. *Las Vegas and Uncle Joe: The New Mexico I Remember.* University of Oklahoma Press, 1964.

CHAPTER 22
TRIBE OF THE WEREWOLF

DID AN ANCIENT TRIBE from the Ohio Valley worship werewolves in some manner? According to a discovery made years ago, this is a disturbing possibility. It all began on a fall afternoon in Eagle Creek, Ohio, in 1949 when local farmer A.C. Ayres was out digging post holes in his field when a glint of metal caught his eye. As he got down to look at it, it appeared to be an old copper wristband jutting out from the wet clay. Although such finds were fairly routine in the Ohio Valley, something told Ayres that this one might be something special. And it was, for it would eventually lead to remains of what appeared to be a human-wolf hybrid.[82]

---

[82] In the years since, paranormal investigators have gone back and forth between wondering whether these were real

ADENA MOUND IN ROSS COUNTY, OHIO, C.1901.

Ayres, who was formerly of Kentucky, decided to contact archaeologist at the University of Kentucky who had previously reached out to farmers in Allen County, telling them to keep an eye out for artifacts from the Ohio Valley mound builders. Ayres, assuming it was perhaps a remnant of the mound builders, contacted them. The archaeologists came and were quite excited by the bracelet. They were even more excited when Ayres took them to the spot where he was digging his post holes, which they quickly identified as a 1500-year-old burial mound from the Adena Culture.

By the spring of 1950, the old burial mounds were being excavated by the university. During the dig, they came across shreds of decomposing fiber, which they assumed was leather. Digging deeper they soon found bones and human remains. The

---

werewolves or simply the remnants of a tribe who worshiped werewolves.

skeleton, from the best that they could piece together, they determined was that of a very large man who had been killed in the prime of his life.

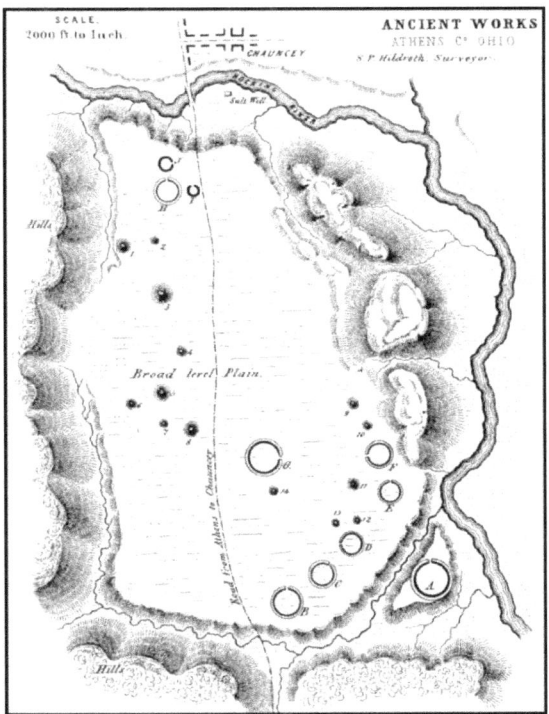

WOLF PLAINS GROUP c.1848.

The body had been enshrouded in the leather remnant they had first found. However, they wondered why the skull of the man had been so violently crushed. Along with the other remains, the fragments of the skull were taken to the university to be reassembled. And that's when things got really strange. Part of the head comprised the cut jawbone of a wolf. The jawbone had been intricately carved to fit a hollowed out space within the man's own jawbone. Something similar had been found ten years earlier in Montgomery County, Kentucky. It, too, had puzzled the anthropologists until now.

After a thorough study, the archaeologists figured out that in life, the deceased man had had his front teeth purposefully removed and replaced with those of a wolf.

The anthropologists soon began speculating about what it meant to the Adena religion. Did, perhaps, some of their arcane ceremonies involve a wolf cult? Did others have their teeth taken out and replaced with those of wolves? Furthermore, anthropologists were certain that the body found in Ohio was that of a tribal leader, chief, or medicine man. They determined this because few in that culture were given the honor of a single burial in a mound (usually, the mounds were mass burials).

Lastly, as opposed to going through life with the wolf's teeth in his mouth, some speculated that perhaps the wolf teeth were placed in his mouth post-mortem.

Sources:
Steiger, Brad. *Real Zombies, the Living Dead, and Creatures of the Apocalypse.* Visible Ink Press, 2010.

POSTSCRIPT
UNDEAD ARMY OF SHIPROCK

AMIDST THE MANY LANDMARKS dotting Dinétah, the homeland of the Navajo, Shiprock Peak stands among the tallest, literally and figuratively. Stretching just a little over 1,500 feet into the sky, the formation was so named due to its sailing-ship-like appearance in the distance. In Navajo it is called *Tsé Bit'a'í,* literally meaning *rock with wings.* That name is appropriate, for according to Navajo legend, the peak didn't always reside in New Mexico's San Juan County. The formation was called the "rock with wings" because, according to myth, it literally flew to the spot to transport the Navajo to a new home. Some have likened this story to the "ancient aliens" class of thinking, with the idea being that a spacecraft of some kind transported the Navajo. Others view it simply as a myth, and instead of a craft, Shiprock peak was the remains of a mighty bird monster that had carried the tribe to New Mexico.

Whatever Shiprock originally was, in the early days, the Navajo lived atop the peak for safety, only venturing below to gather food. But then, one day, calamity struck by way of a horrible storm. An intense lightning strike obliterated the bridge allowing access to the peak, and in the process, hundreds of Navajo women and children were left stranded. Lest they disturb their *chindi*, or ghosts, the Navajo today consider the peak sacred and unscalable.

THE EXPEDITION LEAVING FORT WINGATE.
[*Photographed for the "Examiner."*]

ILLUSTRATION FROM THE *SAN FRANCISCO EXAMINER* OF MAY 1, 1892.

A gold strike in the nearby Carrizo Mountains in the year 1890 caused a particularly interesting Navajo legend regarding Shiprock to resurface. In summary, during a blizzard, a group of prospectors had sought out a lost gold mine somewhere on the Navajo Reservation and actually found it on Carrizo Mountain in March of 1890. The Navajo, led by Chief Black Horse, tried and failed to expel the miners. As such, Chief Black Horse traveled to

COWBOYS & ZOMBIES

Fort Wingate to get help from the soldiers that oversaw the reservation. Troops were sent out to arrest the miners, who brought back to civilization proof of their gold-strike. When the news hit, it caused considerable excitement, so much so that there was talk of relocating the Navajo so that the reservation could be thoroughly mined.

SHIPROCK PEAK WITH NAVAJO IN FOREGROUND. (LIBRARY OF CONGRESS)

The *San Francisco Examiner* of May 1, 1892, reported on a government sanctioned expedition from Fort Wingate which explored the Carrizo Mountains and brought back further ore samples of valuable metals. Politicians began talking about dividing up the Navajo reservation so that it could be mined, which naturally upset the Navajo. Worse yet, if the white man found gold on Carrizo Mountain, could the mining of Shiprock Peak be next?

WHERE MAN HAS NEVER TROD,

Government Expedition in Search of a Modern El Dorado.

A TOMB THE NAVAJOS HAVE GUARDED WITH THEIR LIVES.

A Fabled Land of Hills and Mountains of Solid Silver and Gold—Whence No White Prospector Has Ever Returned Alive — The Navajo Legend of the Grave of the Indian "Mother of Life."

FORT WINGATE (N. M.), April 19.—The Mother of Life is to be disturbed. Her tomb is to be profaned by the insulting presence of the white man.

If the white men like the tomb the indications are that they will take it, for the evil spirit of trade has entered the souls of her Navajo warriors, and though they have guarded the tomb of the Mother of Life with their bodies ever since the morning of time, the day seems to be coming when the holy mountains will be traded for fields and pasture lands.

An expedition is now preparing to go from

SAN FRANCISCO EXAMINER (MAY 1, 1892).

COWBOYS & ZOMBIES

Thankfully, this never came to pass. The Navajo kept their sacred lands, and Shiprock Peak went unmolested. As stated before, the scare brought to light an old Navajo legend dating back to the days of Spanish rule and the Conquistadors. Supposedly, Spanish priests had enslaved local Navajos to work a gold mine very near Shiprock in the 16th century.

The *San Francisco Examiner* of May 1, 1892, reported the legend. For context, the *Examiner* referred to Shiprock as "The Tomb of the Mother," and treated the mountain as though it was one of the chief Navajo deities that would one day cause an earthquake to drive away invaders from the sacred Navajo lands. The article related:

There is a tradition that for fifty years the holy ground was not in the possession of the Indians. That must have been about two centuries ago. There is a lost padre mine somewhere in those mountains. The old Spanish Fathers are said to have worked it for generations. According to the story there was a strong army at the mine against which the Navajos could do nothing, for the men wore iron breastplates that their arrows could not pierce. During all this period the mother was restive. For weeks the sun did not come.

Ship Rock mountain and the surrounding country heaved and shook with the mother's indignation. Mountains opened and rivers ceased to run, but the invaders stayed on. At last the turbulence awoke the thunder god and the god that-shakes-the-earth. The mother invoked their aid, and then came a day when the sky opened and let down a deluge, and the mine was crushed between two mountains. Then all the Navajos who had been killed in fighting the invaders were awakened from death by the shaking, so fierce it was, and they fell upon the armored soldiers and drove them into a canyon, from which they could not escape, and rolled down bowlders on them until they were all dead and buried.

Ever since that time the Navajos have been in possession of the Ship Rock peak.

It's unknown if the *San Francisco Examiner* invented this tale of undead warriors for the delight of readers, or if it was a real oral tradition among the Navajo. Regardless of where the story came, it's certainly a fantastic one.

APPENDIX
THE LOST CASES

ORIGINALLY, I INTENDED to call this book "Cowboys & Monsters: The Lost Cases," before "Cowboys & Zombies" emerged as the more appealing title of the two. It is of that aborted title that this appendix was born. In short, the entries to follow are cases I just couldn't get anywhere with because they were frankly a little too weird. Often, they lacked corroborating evidence as well. Think of them as the long expired, back of the fridge items which I threw in for you diehard readers of the strange.

The first story appears to tell of a minotaur, and was printed in the *Titusville Morning Herald* on May 15, 1866, published out of Pennsylvania.

JOHN LEMAY

Ghostly Manifestations

Some vague and ill-defined rumors have reached us of late, concerning a weird and mysterious phenomenon, or a succession of supernatural scenes and *outre* developments, occurring some five or six miles from Middletown, in the town of Mount Hope.[83] For reasons which will readily occur to the reader, the parties immediately affected by these strange demonstrations have been very reticent in the matter, and request that names and locality may be withheld from the public until further investigations shall unravel the mystery, or an adequate cause be assigned for what now seems to be unearthly, if not demoniacal, in its origin.

"Some time in the latter part of March last, the residents of a quiet and humble hamlet, standing near the confines of a densely-wooded lot of some four acres, and near the highway leading to the village of Mount Hope, were awakened from sleep by a novel and singular sound, which at first fell faintly, but defiantly upon the ear. It was as if a large choir, or a multitude of voices, were harmoniously humming, or singing with closed lips, a solemn, funeral dirge, the refrain, after regular intervals of silence, resembling, as near as the sound

---

[83] The article isn't clear in what state this story took place in, but it sounded to be in Delaware due to the mention of Middleton and Mount Hope being in such close vicinity to one another.

could be rendered, the word *zinzah—zinzah—zinzah—* three times repeated, and, after a moments pause, succeeded by the same sad, monotonous murmuring as before. This continued for nearly half an hour, when the awed family were summoned to a display of some of the most discordant and unearthly sighs and groans that ever fell on mortal ears. Every phase of suffering, every expression of mental and physical pain which may be conceived of, was uttered forth with a fierce intensity....

"It is not strange that the animals on the premises shared the wonder and amazement which possessed the people. This was manifested by the mingling of their own particular cries and instinctive utterances with the general discord, thus adding an accompaniment, and chorus to the distracting din, and heightening the pandemonic effect of this diabolical overture.

"Amazement, of course, had now almost found its extreme limit, and the people were prepared for any further change in the sardonic program which the invisible performers might still have in reserve. They had not long to wait. Presently the darkness of midnight suddenly changed to the broad glare of noonday. It was as if a thousand waving festoons of electric light had swooped down from the murky heavens to unfold [we], with gauzy wreaths of flame and tongues of fire, the trunks and limbs of trees barren of foliage. They sparkled and shone now with a wealth of flashing light, and grotesque, but entrancing forms of beauty. Far off, the northern heavens seemed to catch and reflect from horizon to zenith the auroric scene; and evolving, ever-changing banners, of the tint and shades of the rainbow, flaunted up the broad expanse. ... It was soon at midnight! But darkness and silence soon settled upon the earth; the rustling of the trees and low moaning of the winds alone broke the oppressive stillness of the hour.

"But a new and more astounding scene was soon to follow. While the family were exchanging in suppressed and hesitating whispers their surmises, and seeking for some solution of the wonders of which they had been involuntary witnesses, every door in the house was suddenly and violently thrown open by a power unseen, and through the main entrance came stalking, and swaying from side to side, in frightful contortions, an object neither man nor beast, but bearing, in huge and distorted proportions, the shape and form of the upper extremities of the one, and the lower parts, terribly elongated and reeking with mire and filth, and emitting a smell of phosphorous, of the other. The single candle burning upon the mantel went out, and in the darkness which succeeded forth came from the nostril and eye of the monoculous monster a volume of smoke and flame which soon filled the apartment, and so affected the organs of respiration that suffocation seemed to be imminent.

COWBOYS & ZOMBIES

"With a deep guttural groan, and still sending forth his fiery breathings, this Minotaur, man, beast, or demon, lifted his disgusting and scaly digits and, slowly and with provoking deliberation, passed them over the face and person of each member of the affrighted family, with a yell that seemed to shake the building; then from foundation to rafters, leaped through the open door at the rear of the house, rushed into the forest, and was soon lost in its pervading gloom and darkness.

"There was no sleep in that dwelling on this eventful night; and the next morning no traces of the phenomenon could be discerned, except that along the track of the strange visitor were found some small particles resembling crushed lava; and the sulphurous and phosphorescent odor which filled the house was proof positive to the inmates that they had not been dreaming."

In all likelihood, this story was simply cooked up to entertain readers. And with no given names for the witnesses to investigate, this story becomes even less credible. But, just for context, people did claim to see beasts from mythology from time to time. For instance, there is the fairly well-known Goatman of Prince George County, Maryland. In Centerville, Illinois in May of 1963, the local police received a panicked phone call from Mr. James McKinney claiming that he'd just seen an animal that was "...half-man, half-horse," just like the centaurs of old. While one man seeing such a thing can easily be brushed off, the fact that the police received phone calls from close to fifty other residents reporting the same thing is truly incredible. Another centaur was glimpsed in Melbourne, Florida a few years later standing by the side of the highway. With those sightings in mind, there could have been something to the story in the *Titusville Morning Herald* on May 15, 1866.

In *Cowboys & Monsters*, I included a few accounts of people who could start fires with their minds, but here we shall delve into sightings of beings made entirely of fire, such as an entity seen outside of Davenport, Iowa, in a place called Tiskavilla. It was on the early morning of July 15, 1885, when a being completely enveloped in flames made its presence known on a small farm. I have not the exact newspaper source for the story, but the reliable Jerome Clark dug it up and published it in the *Magonia Exchange* project. It goes as follows:

A man named Richardson lived on a small farm near this village. He was industrious and well-liked by his neighbors. On Wednesday of last week his youngest child, a daughter, ran screaming to a neighbor's before daylight, saying that a huge man, all covered with fire, had come into the house and carried off all but her. It was supposed that the house was on fire, and aid was quickly afforded, but the house was found to be all right.

Nothing at all was disturbed, but no one was about. The horse and buggy remained in the stable. The clothing left off by members of the family on going to bed was found where it had been left. The vicinity was thoroughly searched, but without avail. No train had stopped, and no water was near. It seemed as if the ground had opened and swallowed the family up.

A neighbor's family moved into the house to take care of the things and the child and was nearly scared to death the first night. They assert that suddenly the house was filled with a strange white light and the voice of Richardson was heard calling his daughter. She responded and instantly the light disappeared and a great shower of small stones fell upon the roof. The same scene has been enacted nightly since and the whole community is aroused. The child does not appear to be in the least alarmed at the voices.[84]

Preceding that account, a fiery woman was spotted near Newbern, North Carolina in May of 1876. *The Carolina Watchman* reported on the incident in their May 4th edition:

Mr. Thomas Land living in Pamlico county, about 20 miles from this city, reported that on Friday night, after he had retired, he heard his dogs barking furiously in the yard and went to

---

[84] If this story is true at all, then it likely falls into the realm of poltergeist rather than some fiery cryptid humanoid. The biggest giveaway that it's a poltergeist is the stone shower, as stones falling on or being thrown at houses from out of nowhere are part of the poltergeist phenomena.

the back door to ascertain the cause. On opening the door, a sight met his gaze which froze his blood and made each hair stand on end like the quills on the fretful porcupine.

Just in front of him, and probably so close that he could feel the heat, was suspended in the air a large ball of fire, about the size and in the shape of a woman. On his making an exclamation of horror, his wife became alarmed and rushed to the door to see what the matter was. When she discovered "the fire woman" she immediately fainted. After putting his wife on the bed, Mr. Land said, he became so frightened at what he had seen that he lay down and "covered up head and ears." Shortly thereafter the ball of fire passed around his house and although the night was a dark one, Mr. Land says one could see to pick up a pin in any part of the house because of the great flood of light from the "fire woman."

In addition to humanoid fire beings were some inhuman fire beings as well that sounded to either come from Hell itself or from Greek mythology. Both of these stories occurred in the late 1860s in Kentucky. Late in the night hours of February 13, 1866, in Bracken County, Kentucky, a fiery monster attacked a plantation. The article, again unearthed by Jerome Clark, read,

On Monday night the owner of a local plantation and his family had retired to rest when suddenly they were aroused by a great outcry from the Negro quarters, which was immediately to the rear of the house. They heard men, women and children screaming in terror, creating a scene of utter pandemonium. His wife and he sprang from their bed. Their room was illuminated as brightly as by a flood of sunlight, though the light was of a bluish cast.

At first they thought that the Negro cabins were being consumed by fire. They rushed to the windows and beheld a sight that fairly curdled the blood in their veins with horror and filled their hearts with outmost terror. Their daughters, shrieking loudly, ran flying into the room, hysterical with fear. They beheld, standing to the right of the upper cabin, near the fence that separated the Negro's garden from the house yard a creature of gigantic stature, and the most horrifying appearance.

It was nearly as high as the cabin and had a monstrous head not similar in shape to that of an ape, with two short white horns above each eye, and it had long arms, covered with shaggy hair of an ashen hue that terminated in huge paws, not unlike those of a cat, and armed with huge and hooked claws. Its breast was as broad as that of a large sized ox, its legs resembled the front legs of a horse, and only the hoofs were cloven. It had a long tail armed with a dart shaped horn, which it was continually switching about. Its eyes glowed like two living coals of fire, while its nostrils and mouth were emitting sheets of blue colored flame, with a hissing sound, like the hissing of a serpent only a thousand fold louder. Its general color, save the arms, was a dull dingy brown. The air was powerfully impregnated with a smell of burning sulfur. The poor Negroes were evidently laboring under extreme terror, and two of them, an old woman and a lad were actually driven to insanity by their fears and have not recovered their reason up to this writing.

The strange creature then was enveloped in a spiral column of flame that reached nearly to the top of the locust trees adjacent, and which hid its horrid form completely from view. The extinction of the flame was instantaneous, and with its disappearance they were relieved of the presence of this remarkable visitor. It was reported that the same or similar creature appeared on several nights at neighboring plantations."

Two years later, another fiery monster visited Bracken County, Kentucky, which can mean one of two things. Either a reporter enjoyed making up stories involving mythological monsters in the area, or the area has a portal to Hell somewhere. (Or a stargate if that's the terminology you prefer.)

On October 10, 1868, a half-man half-horse appeared in the vicinity of Willow Creek. It was over six-feet tall and had "curls of fire falling down over its shoulders." It held a torch in one hand and a sword in another. The tail was said to be composed of three feet of burning flame. It appeared semi-regularly to different witnesses in a spot two miles from Brooksville.

Of course, one has to wonder if these tales were inspired by European folklore? Naturally, there were a few similar stories. One came out of Germany back in the 12th Century and appeared in Volume 1 of the *Deutsche Sagen* (German Legends) from the Brothers Grimm. The book reported on a fiery humanoid on page 229 seen in the year 1125, described as a "fiery man... haunting the mountains like an apparition." The next account of a fire being came courtesy of Abbot Ralph of Essex in his *Chronicles*, which tells of the strange, fiery footprints in York, England in 1189-99: "In the time of King Richard I, of England, there appeared in a certain grassy, flat ground human footprints of extraordinary length; and everywhere the footprints were impressed the grass remained as if scorched by fire." Six years later, in July of 1205, "monstrous tracks were seen in several places, and of a kind never seen before. Men said they were the prints of demons."

Next up comes a merman tale from the *Philadelphia Times* of November 22, 1896:

SHOT A STRANGE MARINE MONSTER
A PARTY OF PORPOISE HUNTERS
CAPTURE A MERMAN.
AN EXTRAORDINARY PRIZE

It Was Only Stunned by the Shot and Nearly Capsized the Boat-A Strange Looking Creature—It is to be Presented to the British Museum.

JOHN LEMAY

From the Washington Pont.

What appears to-be a genuine merman was brought into this port last week by a party of Englishmen. They had been porpoise fishing in the Pacific and were more than confounded at the extraordinary creature they captured. They came in with their prize, fully convinced that the old stories about mermaid and merman were all true, in spite of the scoffers. The man who deserves the credit of this wonderful discovery is Major W. E. Thorncliff, of the British army. The major was at first rather averse to giving the details of his novel adventure, fearing that he would be classed with the spinners of ordinary fish yarns of Puget Sound, but knowing that his social and official position put his word above question, he finally consented to relate his unique experience and to exhibit his interesting captive, only stipulating that I should repeat the facts exactly as he stated them, and describe the sea monster precisely as it really is.

This is the story of the major's adventure in his own words:

"Our party, which consisted of several English noblemen, a French statesman and a Russian prince, left Hokondach, Japan, on a fishing and hunting expedition to the coast, on hoard of prince Gerenoff's steam yacht Anedamoff, on June 20, and we cruised along the shores of the Aleutian Peninsula, calling into many very fine bays and harbors along the coast.

"We shot on shore and fished in the waters of both Behring Sea and the Pacific Ocean, and have as trophies a fine collection of pelts, as well as skeletons of many rare creatures.

"But the climax of all came on the morning of July 20, when we were off the Island of Watmoff. Our men sighted a school of porpoises, among which could be seen several white ones.

"Our hunting boat was lowered and Lord Devonshire, the Earl and I, with the boat's crew, put off from the yacht, determined to capture some of the rare sea pigs. After pulling about four miles we found ourselves in the centre of the school, and Lord Devonshire got a shot at one of the white boys with a large express rifle, which quickly I ended its career.

"Just as we were putting our guns away the Earl called out, 'See that,' pointing to a most startling-looking beast not more than a cable's length away. Picking up his express he fired point blank at it, striking the creature between the eyes. The shot, though it did not kill it, so stunned it that it lay perfectly still on the surface of the sea.

"As our boat hauled along side we saw the most hideous and uncanny-looking monster probably that human eyes ever looked upon. Although at a distance it might perhaps be mistaken for a porpoise, as we came near we saw that it could be truly described by no other name than that of 'merman.'

"As we reached over the side of the boat to haul the creature in it regained some of its vitality. It caught the boat by the gunwale amidship, and had it not been for the fact that when the arms came up out of the sea we naturally shrank to the other side of the boat, it would, without doubt, have capsized us. One of the men picked up an axe and quickly dispatched the monster.

"The better way now would be for you to come with me and I will show you the strange creature which I am now taking to England to present to the British Museum. After seeing it you will, I am sure, be inclined to the opinion that once it is placed there it will easily outrank all of the many strange things to be found in that great repository of the world's rarities."

Then the major led the way to a store room, on Pacific avenue, where, in the middle of the floor, was a large coffin-shaped box. It was 10 feet long, 3 feet wide and 3 feet deep. Taking a screwdriver the major unfastened the top. All that could be seen was some ice, covered with a white woolen blanket. Taking the blanket by the end he quickly removed it and as he did so the sight of the contents almost froze my blood, for right before my eyes was apparently the naked body of a large man.

The major then removed the cloth which covered the lower part of the body. This is exactly the same as that of an ordinary porpoise. The monster is one of the most remarkable freaks nature ever put together. The strange monstrosity measures ten feet from its nose to the end of its fluke-shaped tall, and the girth of its human-shaped body was just six feet.

It would weigh, it is estimated, close to 500 pounds. From about the breast bone to a point about where the base of the stomach would be, were it human. It looked exactly like a man. Its arms, quite human in shape and form, are very long and covered completely with long coarse, dark reddish hair, as is the whole body.

It had or did have at one time four fingers and a thumb on each hand, almost human in shape, except that in place of finger nails there were long, slender claws. But in days long since gone by it had evidently fought some monster that had got the best, of it, for the forefinger of the right hand, the little finger of the left and the left thumb are missing entirely.

Immediately under the right breast is a broad, ugly looking scar, which looked as if some time in the past it had been inflicted by a swordfish. On the sides and body of the monster are numerous other evidences that its life in the ocean had been far from a placid one. There is hardly a space the size of one's hand that does not show evidence of having at some time or other received wounds.

When the hideous body reaches England that country can safely say that it possesses the strangest freak the mysterious waters of the pacific ever gave up.

"Now, mind," was Major Thorncliff's parting salutations, "don't in any way try to embellish what you have seen and heard, but just tell the plain facts, and though this coast may be renowned for strange and weird stories, this story of the merman, simply and truthfully told, will, I am confident, prove the adage. 'Truth is stranger than fiction." Now, it only remains for some man as responsible and well known as Major Thorncliff to discover the mate of the merman, and we will be convinced that the old mariners had not, after all, the wonderful powers of imagination and romance so long ascribed to them.

From the *St. Tammany Farmer*, of Covington, Louisiana, on October 26, 1878, came a story of a hairy lizard-man:

Wild Man of the Woods.
A FEARFUL PRODIGY CAPTURED IN THE WILDS OF TENNESSEE AND BROUGHT TO LOUISVILLE FOR EXHIBITION – HIS BODY COVERED WITH FISH SCALES.

The wild man brought to the city yesterday by Dr. O. G. Broyler, of Sparts, Tenn., is truly a mysterious and wonderful creature. He will be exhibited throughout the country by Manager Whallen, of the Metropolitan, who is a third-owner is this remarkable being, who promises to successfully baffle all scientists who desire to give a satisfactory explanation of his unnatural appearance. Before entering into the details of his capture, which form quite a thrilling and interesting episode, a description of the curiosity, which promises to excite more attention than Barnum's "What Is It?" will be given. At a distance the general outline of his figure would indicate that he is only an ordinary man. Close inspection shows that his whole body is covered with a layer of scales, which drop off at regular periods in the spring and fall, like the skin of a rattlesnake.

He has a heavy growth of hair on his head, and a dark, reddish beard about six inches long. His eyes present a frightful appearance, being at least twice the size of the average sized eye. Some of his toes are formed in an altogether strange appearance, which give his feet a strange appearance, and his height, when standing perfectly erect, is about six feet five inches.

A nervous twitching of his muscles shows a desire to escape, and he is constantly looking in the direction of the door through he entered. His entire body must be wet at intervals, and should this be neglected he begins to manifest great uneasiness, his flesh becomes feverish, and his snifferings cannot be alleviated until the water is applied, and yesterday morning when Mr. Wallen attempted to place him in wagon, in which he intended to bring him to the theatre, it occupied some time. The strange creature acted in the most mysterious manner, refusing obstinately for some time to get into the wagon.

He has quite a sharp appetite, having eaten a meal yesterday morning that would have fully satisfied at least four men. With the exception of fish, his meals are all prepared in the ordinary way, but the fish is eaten entirely raw. Dr. Broyler says that when alone he will sometimes mutter an unintelligible jargon, which it would be impossible for any one to understand, but that, in the presence of visitors, he remains perfectly silent.

Yesterday afternoon, from one to four, a private exhibition was given, and a number of physicians were present, among them Drs. Brady and Cary Blackburn, who said that he was a great curiosity. Dr. Blackburn said that his scaly condition could not be attributed to any skin disease, but undoubtedly he was born in that condition. He will be on exhibition in the private rooms of the Metropolitan Theatre this afternoon and to-morrow between the hours of one and four o'clock. Only physicians and those specially invited will be allowed admission.

His exact age is not known, but for the past eighteen years he has been running wild in the Cumberland mountains in Tennessee, near the Caney Fork and Big Bone Creek. He has been the constant terror of the community, although he was never known to attack any one until the day of his capture.

Dr. G.G. Broyler, of Sparta, Tenn., says that since the surrender of the Confederate army it has been his intention to capture this creature and exhibit him throughout the country. The doctor says the parents of the wild man are respectable citizens of North Carolina, named

Creslin. That their son is unquestionably a mysterious freak of nature they did not deny, but they could not account for his scaly skin. At the tender age of five years, having always been possessed with a roving disposition, he left his home and plunged immediately into the mountainous regions of Tennessee. Here he lived as best he could, subsisting on the products of the country, such as roots and herbs and small animals that he could capture. When in the water he was in his element. He would dive down into the dept of the inland lakes, remaining under water for a considerable length of time, and finally emerge with both hands filled with small fish, which he would devour at once in the raw state.

Dr. Broyler says that until about eighteen months ago he had not attempted the capture, although he had been watching the creature's actions for the past twelve years. About the 15th of September he started into the mountains fully determined to succeed in the capture.

The "Wild Man of the Woods," as he was termed by the people of the vicinity, was unusually fleet of foot and possessed of a great deal of agility, bounding over the mountainous ravines in the most fearless manner. During the chase they kept the wild man constantly in sight, and their plan was to tire him out, in which they finally succeeded.

He was pursued through the wild mountainous country, over lakes and precipices, until his pursuers almost despaired of success. Stratagem was finally resorted to. The lariat was thrown at him without success, and then a kind of net trap was formed, into which he was decoyed and captured. He ran fearlessly into the net, and became entangled in the meshes.

Captured, but not conquered, a struggle ensued, in which Dr. Broyler was seriously wounded. The wild man fought with his hands after the fashion of a bear, and bruised and scratched the doctor in a frightful manner. At last they quieted their unwilling victim and brought him to Sparta. The doctor immediately telegraphed to Mr. Whallen, who purchased a third interest in the wonder and had him brought to Louisville yesterday morning. The presence of the wild man in Louisville has excited considerable attention among the doctors, and also a large crowd of curious persons who are anxious to see the wonderful creature. There will be only one exhibition in this city, which takes place at the Metropolitan Theatre Saturday evening.

From the *St. Louis Missouri Globe-Democrat,* notorious for odd tales, came this one of another lizard-like humanoid. If there's any truth to it at all worth speculating over, the only thing it sounds like to me would be a Reptilian-type alien. Anyhow, it was published on January 17, 1885:

Some hunters were startled a few days ago by the appearance of an uncouth, horrible-looking animal, south of the O. & M. Railroad Bridge over Fox River near Olney. They had killed but little game, and were consoling each other over their bad luck, when their attention was attracted by a noise to the top of a fallen tree, and looking up they beheld a monster such as they had never seen before.

They describe the beast as the ugliest looking animal they ever saw. Its head and face resembled that of a dark-skinned human, with a very large mouth full of sharp, fang-like teeth. Its neck was two or three feet long and covered with short red colored hair; its body was five or six feet in length, and was covered with scales and looked bright like those of a sunfish; its tail was three or four feet long and curved up over its back; its legs were short and the feet webbed, and the toes had long claws.

One of the hunters, who got too near in trying to throw a rope over its head, was struck by the animal's tail, and he tumbled headlong twenty feet away. The animal then made for the creek and disappeared. The beast had been devouring a hog. A party has been organized for the capture of this wild animal. The parties who describe it are good men and perfectly reliable.

An article published in the *Petersburg Daily Index* on December 18, 1868, told of a demonic monster loose on the farm of Silas Brown (an alias given to the witness). For several weeks, Brown was accosted by a monster when he went out at night to feed his horses.

[Mr. Brown] who lived at the edge of a wooded area, reported that for the last few weeks he has had visions or encountered an alarming character in the nearby forest but more particularly in the copse adjacent to Mr. Brown's barn and stable. At numbers of times has an immense figure been seen passing to and fro near the barn, with large horns and terrible claws, which it contracts to a sort of hoof, and has assaulted Mr. Brown, when he attempted after dark to feed his horses and stock, in such a manner and with such violence that he has been compelled to flee to his house for safety.

The figure, to the best of Mr. Brown's recollection seemed about three times as large as a man in its front, and having a back converging from its neck and shoulders horizontally to the distance of some six to eight feet, and supplied on each side with huge and tremendous arms. It is of a pale bluish color when first seen, but upon being irritated by the near approach of any person becomes a deadly white, and issues from its surface a small volume of smoke, accompanied with a sickening smell. This ghoul or unnatural and horrible animal or demon, has been seen as often as four times near Mr. Brown's stable, and when seen, it has lingered till its deadly effluvia has completely impregnated the surrounding atmosphere.

One evening Mr. Brown, desiring to have another beside himself see this terrible visitant, induced a courageous gentleman called Siger, who happened with his wife to spend the evening at Mr. Brown's to go to the stable to feed his horses. Siger, not believing the story, went without hesitation, when, upon entering the stable, he was alarmed by the fall at or near his feet, with a deep rumbling sound, of a tremendous stone. Siger without looking to see whence the rock came, picked the stone up, and it was so hot that he was compelled to drop it.

Upon looking up he beheld the unearthly monster not over fifty yards from him, and the air became quickly filled and inoculated with brimstone. Not wishing to be thought a coward, he did not mention anything of this at the house, but upon walking home with his wife the same night he told her of what happened at the stable, and instantly she became alarmed, and was carried home in a state of apparent insensibility.

The neighborhood is in a terrible state of excitement, and steps have been taken to investigate this frightening matter.

The *Lake Charles Echo* of May 3, 1879, reported the strange story of "A Boy-Rooster."

The strangest freak of nature on record has just come to light in the shape of a "boy-rooster." The parents of the strange malformation, now about six years old, from mortification, kept its existence a profound secret except in a few instances where near relatives were permitted to see it, until recently when it was taken to St. Louis to see if the learned doctors could account for its strange deformity, but they could not. This strange creature was born or hatched about ten miles from Vicksburg, in Mississippi.

The head and feet of this strange creature is as perfect a chicken as was ever hatched, while its hands and body is that of a perfect human, except that its hands are as large as those of a man. It has beak, comb and gills like a chicken, and its neck from its head to its shoulders is covered with beautiful red feathers tinged with gold, and it crows and talks alternately.

It has the intellect of the human, but when it comes to its food it will eat nothing except such food as fowls feed upon, and is extremely fond of bugs and worms, which it catches out in the yard, and says they are perfectly splendid. It is a great cross to its mother to see it out in the yard catching worms. The name of the father of this boy-rooster is Rathbone.

This is certainly the most wonderful child that the world has ever seen. Barnum would doubtless give a half million dollars for it, but its parents say that they cannot afford to make money out of the misfortunes of their offspring, and will not even exhibit it for pay.

The *West-Jersey Pioneer* of October 15, 1859, told of what they deemed a half-woman half-pig:

From an authentic source, which forbids us to doubt the truth of the story, the following facts have been received: One day week before last, the passengers on board a ferry boat, near

Quebec, were attracted by the singular appearance of a woman who occupied a rather secluded position, and who seemed to be under the care of some persons who acted as if anxious to shield her from observation. Her arms were bandaged, but not so closely as to prevent a constant and very unusual motion; and her head, which was completely covered and hidden from sight, was observed to sway incessantly backward and forward beneath the folds of cloth. As soon as the ferry boat reached the shore, the figure was conveyed to the train of cars in waiting, and seated therein; but at this moment a sort of struggle and tumult again attracted the notice of the bystanders, and the car was filled with eager inquiries. Those who entered, however, hastily returned, their faces pallid with horror.

Among them was the conductor of the train, who begged that no one would approach, for the bandage had been thrown off, and it had been discovered that the creature was a monster possessing the form of a woman, except the head and arms, which were those of a pig. No mere human resemblance, but the absolute fact. This would seem incredible, were it the only case of this kind. It is known, however, that there lived in Albany, N.Y., a few years ago, a similar creature, having a woman's body and a pig's head; in this instance the arms were human. This being was always kept in close confinement, and never suffered to leave a certain room in the house, where those who had charge of her resided, excepting when no visitors were about. She could talk imperfectly, and was capable of some degree of mechanical labor, for her sewing was said to be very beautiful. Her head was in every respect that of a pig, no particular was wanting - ears, bristles, even tusks, all were there. This creature died at the age of thirty five years, after having been for some time destitute of the little reason she once had.

The Caucasian of September 19, 1907, out of Louisiana told of a real life Gorgon in the sense that it was a "snake woman":

Peculiar Creature Which
Party Seeks to Capture.

Jamestown, Va., Sept. 19. - An expedition has started from this city, headed by several veteran mountaineers, having for its object the investigation of a weird tale regarding a snake woman who, it is alleged, frequents the wild parts of the moonshine country.

This strange creature who, several witnesses have declared, resembles a reptile as much as a woman, will be captured if it is possible for the members of the expedition to catch a glimpse of her. A mountaineer on a visit to Jamestown brought the first story of the snake woman and claimed to be one of the very few people who had actually seen her.

COWBOYS & ZOMBIES

For years, he stated, tales of a wild woman with the skin of a snake, who traveled upon the ground like a reptile and subsisted upon living prey, have been told, but these tales were generally regarded as idle rumors. Stone Colby, a grizzled mountaineer who visited the exposition, however, declares that the stories, instead of being exaggerated, only tell half the truth about the strange woman. It was he who made the offer to lead an expedition to the place where the woman lives.

Covered with the scaly skin of a snake and shedding it regularly once a year in one piece, the snake woman glides among the trees and rocks in search of small animals, mice, frogs, ground squirrels and other forest and swamp prey, which Stone has seen her eat alive, swallowing them like a reptile, without mastication.

INDEX

COWBOYS & ZOMBIES

COWBOYS & ZOMBIES

ABOUT THE AUTHOR

John LeMay was born and raised in Roswell, NM, the "UFO Capital of the World." He is the author of over 50 books on film and western history such as *Kong Unmade: The Lost Films of Skull Island*, *Tall Tales and Half Truths of Billy the Kid*, and *Roswell USA: Towns That Celebrate UFOs, Lake Monsters, Bigfoot and Other Weirdness*. In addition to non-fiction, he is also the author of the novels *The Noted Desperado Pancho Dumez* and *Once Upon a Time in Fort Sumner* both of which utilize folklore of the Southwest. He has written for magazines such as *True West*, and writes regularly for newspapers and journals like *The Tombstone Epitaph* and *The Wild West History Association Journal*. He is a Past President of the Board of Directors for the Historical Society for Southeast New Mexico.

THE BICEP BOOKS CATALOGUE

The following titles are available for purchase on Amazon.com, and are available to bookstores at a wholesale discount via Ingram Content Group (ISBNs of available editions listed for this purpose)

CRYPTOZOOLOGY/COWBOYS & SAURIANS

Cowboys & Saurians: Prehistoric Beasts as Seen by the Pioneers explores dinosaur sightings from the pioneer period via real newspaper reports from the time. Well-known cases like the Tombstone Thunderbird are covered along with more obscure cases like the Crosswicks Monster and more. Softcover (357 pp/5.06" X 7.8") Suggested Retail: $19.95 ISBN: 978-1-7341546-1-0

Cowboys & Saurians: Ice Age zeroes in on snowbound saurians like the Ceratosaurus of the Arctic Circle and a Tyrannosaurus of the Tundra, as well as sightings of Ice Age megafauna like mammoths, glyptodonts, Sarkastodons and Sabertoothed tigers. Tales of a land that time forgot in the Arctic are also covered. Softcover (264 pp/5.06" X 7.8") Suggested Retail: $14.99 ISBN: 978-1-7341546-7-2

Southerners & Saurians takes the series formula of exploring newspaper accounts of monsters in the pioneer period with an eye to the Old South. In addition to dinosaurs are covered Lizardmen, Frogmen, giant leeches and mosquitoes, and the Dingocroc, which might be an alien rather than a prehistoric survivor. Softcover (202 pp/5.06" X 7.8") Suggested Retail: $13.99 ISBN: 978-1-7344730-4-9

Cowboys & Saurians South of the Border explores the saurians of Central and South America, like the Patagonian Plesiosaurus that was really an lemisch, plus tales of the Neo-Mylodon, a menacing monster from underground called the Minhocao, Glyptodonts, and even Bolivia's three-headed dinosaur! Softcover (412 pp/ 5.06"X7.8") Suggested Retail: $17.95 ISBN: 978-1-953221-73-5

UFOLOGY/THE REAL COWBOYS & ALIENS IN CONJUNCTION WITH ROSWELL BOOKS

The Real Cowboys and Aliens: Early American UFOs explores UFO sightings in the USA between the years 1800-1864. Stories of encounters sometimes involved famous figures in U.S. history such as Lewis and Clark, and Thomas Jefferson. Hardcover 242pp/6" X 9") Softcover (262 pp/5.06" X 7.8") Suggested Retail: $24.99 (hc)/$15.95(sc) ISBN: 978-1-7341546-8-9\(hc)/978-1-7344 730-8-7(sc)

The second entry in the series, *Old West UFOs*, covers reports spanning the years 1865-1895. Includes tales of Men in Black, Reptilians, Spring-Heeled Jack, Sasquatch from space, and other alien beings, in addition to the UFOs and airships. Hardcover (276 pp/6" X 9") Softcover (308 pp/5.06" X 7.8") Suggested Retail: $29.95 (hc)/$17.95(sc) ISBN: 978-1-7344730-0-1 (hc)/ 978-1-73447 30-2-5 (sc)

The third entry in the series, *The Coming of the Airships*, encompasses a short time frame with an incredibly high concentration of airship sightings between 1896-1899. The famous Aurora, Texas, UFO crash of 1897 is covered in depth along with many others. Hardcover (196 pp/6" X 9") Softcover (222 pp/5.06" X 7.8") Suggested Retail: $24.99 (hc)/$15.95(sc) ISBN: 978-1-7347816 -1-8 (hc)/978-1-7347816-0-1(sc)

Featuring cases the authors missed, *The Lost Cases* covers things such as the skyquakes recorded by Lewis and Clark, airships and the Spanish American War, Pancho Villa and crystal skulls, lost alien tribe of the Tundra, invisible alien monsters, the Great Moon Hoax of 1835, hellhounds and airships, the Sonora Airship Club and more. Softcover (252 pp/5.06" X 7.8") Suggested Retail: $18.99 ISBN: 978-1-953221-55-1

COWBOYS & SAURIANS CONT'D

Cowboys & Saurians: Dinosaurs Down Under takes the series to Australia to explore tales of the cattle devouring Burrunjor, the dreaded Diprotodon, the terrible Tantanoola Tiger, the marsupial Sasquatch known as the Yowie, plus Thylacines, Bunyips, giant rabbits, Megalodons and dinosaurs in nearby New Zealand. Softcover (240 pp/ 5.06" X 7.8") Suggested Retail: $14.95 ISBN: 978-1-953221-34-6

As the title suggest, *Cowboys & Saurians in the Modern Era* takes the series into the 20th Century with tales of the Texas Pterosaur flap of 1976, the Bladenboro Beast of the 1950s, the Busco Turtle Beast of the 1940s, dinosaur sightings in the Great Depression and far out tales of mini-mastodons, dinosaur men, and Snallygasters. Softcover (320 pp/ 5.06" X 7.8") Suggested Retail: $19.95 ISBN: 978-1-953221-22-3

Settlers & Serpents wrangles the best "Snaik Stories" of the Southwest and beyond in a single volume. Whether it's simple giant snakes or lake serpents, they're corralled in the pages within. Also included are entries on the Leviathan in Mesoamerica and the Southwest plus a detailed look at the giant rattlesnake of Pecos Pueblo. Softcover (180 pp/ 5.06" X 7.8") Suggested Retail: $14.59 ISBN: 978-1-953221-21-6

Written for young readers ages 9-12, *Monsters of the Old South* collects the best creature stories of the swamplands including the White River Monster, Green Eyes, the Crocodingo, the Averasboro Gallinipper, the Tennessee Snake Woman, the Arkansas Gowrow, Bigfoot in the Mississippi River and more. Softcover (122 pp/4.25" X 7") Suggested Retail: $12.99 ISBN: 978-17347816-9-4

THE REAL COWBOYS & ALIENS CONT'D

Early 20th Century UFOs kicks off a new series that investigates UFO sightings of the early 1900s. Includes tales of UFOs sighted over the *Titanic* as it sunk, Nikola Tesla receiving messages from the stars, an alien being found encased in ice, and a possible virus from outer space!Hardcover (196 pp/6" X 9") Softcover (222 pp/5.06" X 7.8") Suggested Retail: $27.99 (hc)/$16.95(sc) ISBN: 978-1-7347816-1-8 (hc)/978-1-73478 16-0-1(sc)

UFOs in the Roaring Twenties takes a look at UFO sightings in the 1920s just as the title suggests, along with accounts of Mothman in Nebraska, Lincoln LaPaz's first UFO case, Men in Black investigating an airship crash in Braxton County, West Virginia, Camden's Cosmic Sniper, and much more! Softcover (248 pp/5.06" X 7.8") Suggested Retail: $19.99 ISBN: 978-1-953221-51-3

UFOs of the Turbulent Thirties concludes the authors' investigation of the last unexplored decade of Ufology in the Great Depression with accounts of Mothman, Ghost Fliers, Nazi Bells, the Underground City of the Lizard People, a vanished village on the tundra, and even gangsters and aliens. Softcover (212 pp/5.06" X 7.8") Suggested Retail: $17.95 ISBN: 978-1-953221-35-3

Written for young readers ages 9-12, *Space Monsters of the Old West* collects the best alien sightings of the Wild West including Mummies from Mars, Bigfoot from the Moon, Pascagoula's space ghouls, the Crawfordsville Monster, Spring-Heeled Jack, Blobs from space, and even the dinosaurian alien creatures that invaded Van Meter, Iowa. Softcover (120 pp/4.25" X 7") Suggested Retail: $12.99 ISBN: 978-1-953221-87-2

BICEP BOOKS HISTORY

COWBOYS & MONSTERS

Cowboys & Monsters features potentially true stories of real vampires, werewolves, and even mummies unique to America's Wild West period. Examples include the cursed mummy of John Wilkes Booth, New Orleans immortal vampire Jacques St. Germain, precursors to the Beast of Bray Road, and the origins of Skinwalker Ranch. Softcover (316 pp/5.06" X 7.8") Suggested Retail: $19.99 ISBN: 978-1-953221-46-9

The first entry in this trilogy of non-fiction terror sinks its teeth into the lore of the vampire in North America and Mexico, with detailed rundowns on the vampire hunters of Exeter, Rhode Island, a tribe of Bat People, the nocturnal shape-shifting vampire witches of Tlaxcala, the immortal ways of Comte St. Germain in New Orleans and more. Softcover (200 pp/5.06" X 7.8") Suggested Retail: $12.99 ISBN: 978-1-953221-38-4

Mummies of the Americas explores Death Valley's city of the Dead, King Tut's Tomb along the Arkansas, the Egyptian City of the Grand Canyon plus the famous mummies of John Wilkes Boothe, Elmer McCurdy, the Cardiff Giant, the Mummy of Helldorado, and even Billy the Kid's pickled trigger finger! Softcover (200 pp/5.06" X 7.8") Suggested Retail: $12.99 ISBN: 978-1-953221-37-7

Cowboys & Dogmen is devoted to tales of werewolves of the Wild West including the dreaded Navajo skinwalker, the Watrous Werewolf, the Beast of the Land Between Lakes, the Hellhounds of El Dorado Canyon, the dreaded Dog Eater, the Wahhoo, the Wolf Man of Versailles, the Michigan Dog-Man and more! Softcover (212 pp/5.06" X 7.8") Suggested Retail: $12.99 ISBN: 978-1-953221-36-0

FICTION/ MISC. HISTORY

The first novel from historian John LeMay weaves a fantastic web of fiction via real life mysteries and legends of New Mexico, namely the puzzling theft and return of Billy the Kid's tombstone in 1976, the legend of the Lost Adams Diggings, the villainous Santa Fe Ring, and the enigmatic Acoma Mesa. Softcover (250 pp/5.5" X 7.5") Suggested Retail: $14.95 ISBN: 978-1-953221-42-1

The year is 1950, and old timers connected to the long-dead outlaw Billy the Kid are turning up murdered in New Mexico. Some blame the killings on the avenging witch of the Navajo nation, the skinwalker, while others think it's no coincidence that a man claiming to be a surviving Billy the Kid is set to meet with the governor soon... Softcover (260 pp/5.5" X 7.5") Suggested Retail: $16.95 ISBN: 978-1-953221-32-2

Roswell, USA, the long-forgotten debut work of John LeMay, is available again and covers the minutia of the infamous Roswell UFO Crash of 1947. Notable chapters include tales of an alien ghost haunting the old airbase, monsters in the nearby Bottomless Lakes, and even a dinosaur sighting outside of town. Softcover (248 pp/6" X 9") Suggested Retail: $14.95 ISBN: 978-0-9817597-5-3

This biography, for the first time ever, tells the history of western journalist Ash Upson, who ghostwrote Pat Garrett's *The Authentic Life of Billy the Kid* in 1882 and also reproduces many of Upson's letters that detailed the harsh realities of frontier life in New Mexico during the turbulent Lincoln County War. Softcover (318 pp/5.5" X 8.5") Suggested Retail: $16.99 ISBN: 978-1953221919

BICEP BOOKS HISTORY

STRANGE WEST MAGAZINE

Debut issue features the disappearance of Ambrose Bierce into the depths of Devil's Cave in Ojinaga during the Mexican Revolution in 1914; Tombstone Thunderbird revisited; the mummy of Heldorado; Jack the Ripper in Arizona; Albert Fountain's lost gold; short story by Dr. John Stamey; interview with Donna Blake Birchell on *Haunted Hotels and Ghostly Getaways of New Mexico*. 72 pp.

Strange West #2 features the history of ghost steers, including Old Ruidoso, the Texas M U R D E R steer, and the story that inspired the "Ghost Riders in the Sky"; Mora Frog Man; Weird FWP; UFO over Coyote Springs by Noe Torres; ghosts and murders in White Oaks by Josh Slatten; Colorado River Dinos; interview with artist Jolyon Yates; excerpt from *Once Upon a Time in Fort Sumner*. 72 pp.

Strange West #3 explores Pecos Pueblo's eternal flame and giant rattlesnake; the mummies of Montezuma Castle, the strange history behind the man who stole Billy the Kid's tombstone; Madstone Madness by Donna Blake Birchell; "The West of the Dead" short story by James Townsend; Lechuza on the loose in Texas; interview with Michael Anthony Giudicissi on *Back to Billy* series. 72 pp.

Strange West #4 features Colorado's lost Caverna del Oro by Mike Olafsen; Cameron Mitchell's unfinished Western *The Dream of Hamish Mose* by Julian DiLorenzo; Bootleg Pony by Donna Blake Birchell; South Valley Specter; "West of the Dead" Part II; the wizard of the Jornada del Muerto; Garden of Eden in Nevada; interview with Josh Slatten of Billy the Kid Historical Coalition. 72 pp.

DEAD HORSE HISTORY

Legend & Lore of the Lost Adams covers the general history of and the many alterations of the tale of the Lost Adams Diggings including those made popular by J. Frank Dobie and Western pulp magazines. Plus, Billy the Kid hunting the canyon; ghostly guardians; ancient cliff dwellings; and supernatural earthquakes. Softcover (186 pp/5.5" X 8.5") Suggested Retail: $19.99 ISBN: 978-1-953221-19-3

New Mexico's Lost Worlds & Enchanted Lands includes trips to Three Rivers Petroglyphs; Mesa Rica's giant burial ground; White Sand's lost city; the Enchanted Mesa; Roswell's Lost River; Chaco Canyon; Urraca Mesa's portal to Hell; White Pueblo of the Malpais; Fort Sumner's Petrified Forest; and the lost Seven Cities of Gold. Softcover (186 pp/5.5" X 8.5") Suggested Retail: $19.99 ISBN: 978-1-953221-18-6

Pueblo Magic in the Land of Montezuma chronicles the obscure and long-forgotten history of Montezuma in the Southwest including his Eternal Flame kept at Pecos Pueblo; the sacred serpent; creation myths of the Papago; the history of Montezuma Well and Montezuma Castle; and the Great White Bat of Sierra Blanca. Softcover Softcover (186 pp/5.5" X 8.5") Suggested Retail: $19.99 ISBN: 978-1-953221-14-8

Apacheria Gold in the Land of Adams is a tribute to similar works by J. Frank Dobic, featuring tales of golden bullets used by the Apache to kill prospectors, a phantom mountain guarded by Bigfoot; plus the lost treasures of Captain Cooney; Doc Thorne; Chief Juh, the Apache Kid, Geronimo, and Mangas Coloradas. Softcover (186 pp/5.5" X 8.5") Suggested Retail: $19.99 ISBN: 978-1-953221-16-2

ALSO AVAILABLE

From the author of *The New Mexico Book of Witches*

LA LLORONA
Her Kith & Kin

JOHN LEMAY

Tales of terror from the Southwest!

ALSO AVAILABLE

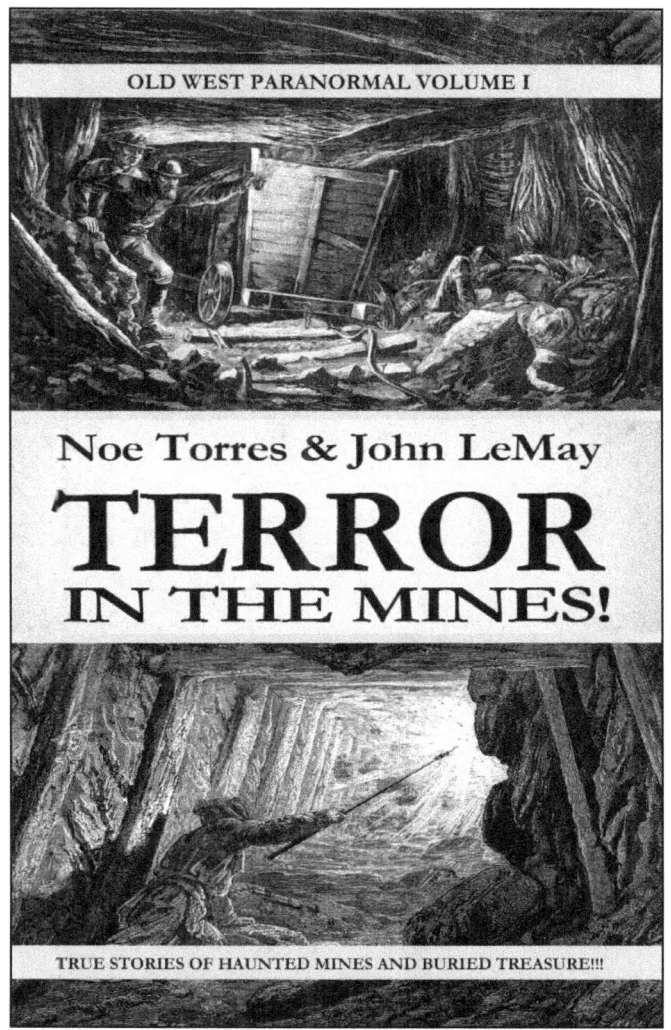

OLD WEST PARANORMAL VOLUME I

Noe Torres & John LeMay

TERROR
IN THE MINES!

TRUE STORIES OF HAUNTED MINES AND BURIED TREASURE!!!

ALSO AVAILABLE

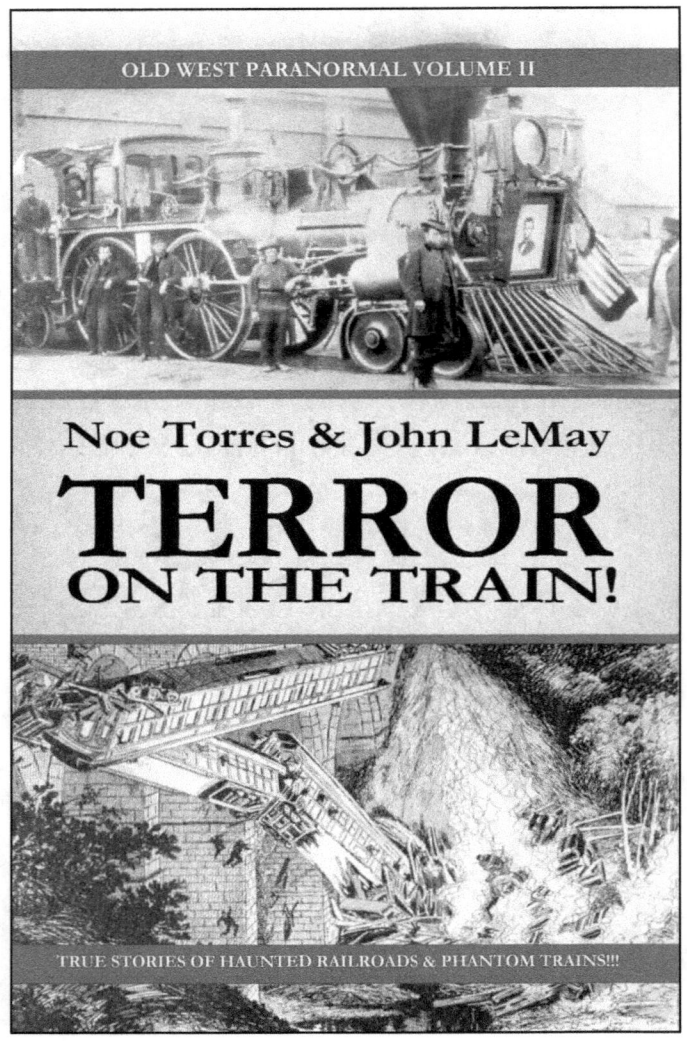

OLD WEST PARANORMAL VOLUME II

Noe Torres & John LeMay

TERROR
ON THE TRAIN!

TRUE STORIES OF HAUNTED RAILROADS & PHANTOM TRAINS!!!

FOR SUPERNATURAL THRILLS, CHECK OUT THE
WESTERN NOVEL, *THE BLACK CANVAS*, FROM
OUR FRIEND MIKE OLAFSON

FOR MORE SUPERNATURAL THRILLS, CHECK OUT
THE WESTERN SHORT STORY COLLECTION,
HITTING THE UNEXPECTED TRAIL, FROM OUR
FRIEND CAROLINE GIAMMANCO